D1328535

THE
ARCHAIC
SMILE
OF
HERODOTUS

Stewart Flory

THE ARCHAIC SMILE OF HERODOTUS

Wayne State University Press   Detroit, 1987

Library of Congress Cataloging-in-Publication Data

Flory, Stewart 1941–
  The archaic smile of Herodotus.

  Bibliography: p.
  Includes index.
  1. Herodotus. History. 2. Herodotus—Technique.
3. Anecdotes. 4. Greece—Historiography. I. Title.
PA4007.F56 1987   938'.0072024   86-32584
ISBN 0-8143-1827-4

To Marleen

CONTENTS

4

ACKNOWLEDGMENTS

I am grateful to the National Endowment for the Humanities for a fellowship in 1982–1983 that allowed me to write the first draft of this book. During that period the American School of Classical Studies at Athens provided an especially hospitable environment as well as an excellent library. I owe special thanks to Steve Miller, Director of the School, and to Nancy Winter and Gerhard Schmidt for unfailing help in the library. Access to the library of the American Academy in Rome has helped me prepare a final draft, and I would like to thank Jim Melchert, Director of the Academy, and Lucilla Marino, the Academy's librarian. In Minnesota the interlibrary loan staff of the Folke Bernadotte Library at Gustavus Adolphus College has helped me enormously. Like all scholars in Minnesota I have profited from the exemplary, state supported Minitex system.

The opportunity to present versions of this text on various occasions over the past several years at meetings of the American Philological Association, the Classical Association of the Midwest and South, and other academic groups has enabled me to sharpen my ideas. I have benefited from the helpful, detailed comments of two anonymous readers, and I am especially grateful for the careful editing of Cathie Brettschneider and Jean Owen, Editor-in-chief of Wayne State University Press, as well as for the support of the Director of the press, Robert Mandel. The footnotes show what I owe to the generations of scholars who have studied Herodotus, but I do not pretend to have mastered the entire bibliography of this vast subject nor do I routinely cite every source merely to agree or disagree.

I continue to owe a great debt for inspiration and encouragement to the late Adam Parry, my teacher and friend of both graduate and undergraduate days at Yale. I owe much to the learning, wit, and kindness of my late colleague at Amherst College, John Andrew Moore, and I have many other friends and colleagues to thank for various kinds of assistance. Among these I want to mention Tom Cole, Bernard Goldman, Janine Genelin, Robert Karsten, Georg Luck, Ed Phinney, and David Porter. Finally I thank my wife and colleague, Marleen Boudreau Flory, for her loving help at every stage of this project.

INTRODUCTION

Only by convention do we assign the name "Histories" to Herodotus' book about the successful Hellenic resistance to Persian aggression in the early fifth century, for we do not know its title, if any, in antiquity. In Herodotus' day the Greek word *historia* meant "inquiry," and there was no one word for what twentieth-century scholars call "history." On the other hand, Cicero had good reason to call Herodotus the "father of history" (*de Legibus* 1.1.5) because Herodotus' book has a clearly historical subject: the clash of great armies, cultures, and ideologies, together with the lives of individuals on either side of the conflict whose personalities and actions shaped events. Herodotus narrates events that actually happened, that left physical traces, and that lived on in the memories of the older generation of the writer's day. Herodotus also displays interest in historical causation, the why and not just the how of what he describes. This interest in causation leads him to begin his book not with the Persian campaign of king Darius against Greece in 490 B.C., but much earlier, in the seventh century, with the growth of the Persian empire. In this way he anticipates the events that led up to the final conflict.

11

Though advocacy or partiality has fallen out of favor as a stance for the historical writer, Herodotus is a "committed" writer. Like Livy or Winston Churchill, he takes sides in the struggle he describes. His Hellenes win, despite numerical inferiority, because they are *better*—more noble, more just, and more deserving of divine favor—than the Persians. Herodotus' narrative thus fits into the pattern of David versus Goliath and "us" versus "them," common standards by which we have continually interpreted events. Nevertheless, even though we may find much of Herodotus old-fashioned and even quaint by modern standards of historical writing, it would be wrong to suggest that he is not a historian. To level such an accusation at the *father* of history would disparage his real and continuing contribution to our understanding of the historical period he describes.

On the other hand, the modern reader who turns to Herodotus for a historical narrative always has difficulty, for the *Histories,* although generally historical in theme and content, seems to fit the category of history only intermittently. True, Herodotus cannot be expected to obey the rules of a genre that had not yet become fully fixed and that he was in the act of creating. In the words of one critic: "There was no Herodotus before Herodotus."[1] Still, Herodotus' *Histories* has, to our eyes, an undeniably patchwork quality, combining factual narrative with anecdotes and anthropological excursuses. The many pages devoted to the customs of primitive tribes and remote peoples do not appear to suit a "historical" narrative but rather seem to belong to an anthropologist's notebook. Speculations on geographical and scientific matters have no apparent connection to the wars between Greece and Persia. Equally "unhistorical" in the *Histories* are the anecdotes—those brief, vivid human dramas encountered on virtually every page. Such is the unforgettable story of Arion, forced to walk the plank by Corinthian pirates and then carried safely to shore on the back of a dolphin (1.24); or the Arabian Nights tale of the clever Zopyrus, who by an elaborate masquerade tricks the Babylonians into opening the gates of their city to his master's army, winning fame and wealth for himself and his descendants

(3.153ff.). These stories add humor, charm, and amusement, but are they true?

Of these two apparently extraneous elements in the *Histories,* the anthropological and the anecdotal, the former seems less reprehensible. Plausible explanation for the anthropological portions has been ready to hand and easy to accept. Scholars have explained these passages by saying that Herodotus began his career as a traveler and raconteur of his own wanderings; only later did he turn to serious history, incorporating his earlier writings, such as the long excursus on Egypt that constitutes Book Two, into the final omnium gatherum that we call the *Histories.*[2] No such easy and plausible explanation, however, offers itself for the anecdotes; not only do they often lack clear links to the historical narrative, but in their style and substance they actually appear *anti*historical, particularly when Herodotus tells an anecdote that he implies or even frankly states did not happen. Some scholars assert that Herodotus tells such stories only because they were told to him, and, even if they seem foolish, he feels an obligation to pass them along to posterity.[3] Herodotus does say on occasion that he is only reporting "what was said to me," and in one famous passage (2.123) he even states that this policy may be understood to apply to his whole book. Herodotus, however, does not claim in this passage that he will report *all* that was said to him. Moreover, to what Herodotus himself says or fails to say about his reporting of anecdotes we may add the practical impossibility of a total recall and record of everything that his informants told him. Some selection among anecdotes, whether conscious or unconscious, is inevitable.

In fact, recent studies have revealed that many of these anecdotes, by themselves apparently frivolous and unconnected to the main narrative, actually repeat specific themes and form patterns. We now, for example, recognize in the *Histories* the motif of the "wise adviser," a man like Solon, Croesus, or Demaratus, who counsels a king and whose good advice is at first approved but then dismissed until it is too late and the predicted calamity has struck.[4] Arion's leap into the sea constitutes one of many examples of the motif of the "brave gesture" by which men show their courageous disregard for death by continuing to pursue their normal style of life even while in the gravest danger.[5] The more we study such anecdotes in which motifs occur, the less remote they clearly are from Herodotus' central narrative and the more they reveal about his ideas about life and his unspoken attitudes to the historical events he describes. The "wise adviser" motif, for example, reveals Herodotus' pessimism about human intelligence—the inability of all those foolish monarchs to follow proven good advice. The "brave gesture" motif, on the other hand, may reveal Herodotus' optimism about the possibilities for heroism. Many of these thematically significant anecdotes, furthermore, occur in the ethnographic sections of the *Histories* and help not only to unify disparate ethnographic accounts but also to tie these sections to the main subject of the book through similarity of theme. The anecdotes, then, by their shared motifs, provide continuity and bring one type of order—that of themes—to the whole work.

The discovery of significant patterns in the anecdotes of the *Histories* has brought a new turn to Herodotean studies. Formerly, scholars explained the anthropological portions by suggesting that the *Histories* is an amalgamation of separate essays composed at various times, reflecting Herodotus' changing and developing interests as a writer: first geography and ethnography, then the chronology of the Persian empire, and finally the history of the Persian wars. For explaining the anecdotal element in the *Histories* there seemed to be only two options: either Herodotus is an undiscriminating naif, or he is actually a serious historian who feels compelled to tell anecdotes to keep a restless audience amused as he reads and lectures aloud.[6] Historians have frequently preferred the former explanation because it preserves a now almost canonical view of Herodotus as a simple, straightforward, almost childlike writer whose inability to organize his material or discriminate among his sources leads him to pass on to us without any alteration the information he heard. According to this way of thinking, Herodotus' very naiveté assures his reliability as a historical source. Against this view of the *Histories* as a primitive, documentary transcript, we can now cite the complexity of the themes that Herodotus weaves through his narrative by means of the anecdotes. Because of our identification of more and more motifs, whose close verbal and thematic correspondences prove deliberate artistry, we can now firmly reject the traditional, unflattering picture of Herodotus as earnest but artless and uncritical.

Thanks to a brilliant insight by Richmond Lattimore, we can also reject the traditional conception of the *Histories* as an amalgam of separate essays in which layers of composition can be distinguished and ranked in order of importance and plausible sequence of composition.[7] Lattimore has proven that our text of the *Histories* is one long, never-revised first draft. When Herodotus wants to correct or modify some statement that he has made, even in the previous sentence, he does not go back to change and revise, thereby producing a new text; rather, according to Lattimore, he makes his correction "in stride," leaving his earlier misstatement to stand. One brief example will serve to demonstrate: Herodotus begins the Croesus story in Book One by saying that this Lydian king was "the first of whom we know" who attacked the Greeks of Asia Minor (1.6.2). Two sentences later Herodotus realizes this statement about Croesus needs qualification since the Cimmerians attacked earlier. Now instead of going back to delete what he has written only two sentences above, he introduces the following correction at the point he has now reached in his manuscript: "Before the reign of Croesus all the Greeks were free, for actually the Cimmerian attack on Ionia was earlier than Croesus—but still the Cimmerians only raided and did not sack cities" (1.6.3). If Herodotus did not care to rewrite even a single sentence, we can scarcely believe that he revised whole chapters and inserted or deleted words, sentences, or paragraphs. The laborious chore of correcting a bookroll or finding the right bookroll to correct among the roughly fifty that we calculate for the *Histories* supports Lattimore's thesis, for Herodotus' book was gigantic at a time when even much shorter books were rare and cumbersome.

The immense length of the *Histories*, which I have suggested elsewhere was very likely the longest book of its day and for some time to come, also allows us to argue against the opinion that Herodotus' anecdotes belong to an utterly separate genre and have a less serious intent than the historical narrative.[8] I reject the view, in other words, that Herodotus tells anecdotes to entertain an audience. Herodotus' book is much too long ever to have been performed for a large audience, and there is no logic in saying he went to the trouble of such lengthy composition only to recite excerpts. Herodotus must have aimed at a relatively small and elite audience of readers. The anecdotes may be amusing, but they are not therefore separate from the *Histories* either in purpose or in composition; nor can we dismiss the ethnographic portions as irrelevant survivals of the author's earlier career. Herodotus must have intended all to go together, and although the *Histories* may have taken months or years to write out, it is patently the result of the same single, ongoing creative urge.

My aim in writing the present book is to argue that the *Histories* is a unified work of art of considerable complexity, coinciding in many respects with the modern genre of history but not precisely classifiable in any modern genre. My thesis is that the anecdotes hold this work together, both in practical terms by repeating the same themes in sections of the book that at first appear unrelated, and in philosophical terms because the repeated themes illuminate the whole historical narrative and the mind of the author. Such a thesis may not find a friendly hearing among those who find literature and history in opposition by nature: "In fiction the principles are given, to find the facts; in history the facts are given, to find the principles."[9] But Herodotus' *Histories* is a unique book composed under unique circumstances as Greek society passed from an oral to a written culture. Herodotus stands alone, midway between the two cultures, oral and written: his book was definitely composed and written for readers, but its substance and its approach are largely oral. It exhibits all the principles of style and organization—such as ring composition, catalogues, and preference for concrete illustration over abstract formulation—that we can identify in Homer and other oral "literatures." I hope, therefore, that the reader will accept the need of a special poetics to understand Herodotus. As for those who believe that to accept Herodotus' literary art is to diminish his historical authority, I hope this book will influence them to think otherwise.

The literary qualities of the *Histories* have attracted comparatively little scholarly attention.[10] The very title *Histories* has dictated the critical approach. The first task of the literary critic of Herodotus' book, then, is to identify related anecdotes by theme and verbal echoes, a task that provides a vast new area for research, so many are the anecdotes and so multifarious their interconnections. A complete catalogue, along the lines of Stith Thompson's *Motif-Index of Folk-Literature,* might be useful, although identification of specific themes (only some of them from folktales) would ultimately be somewhat subjective, since multiple themes often appear in each anecdote.[11] No doubt some anecdotes are "just for fun," but to find out which they are will require much further study. I cannot claim here to have covered every significant literary theme in Herodotus. Some have been studied already, some will be addressed here, but many other themes await exploration, and I hope reading this book will inspire others to help us better understand this deceptively artless artist.

My intent here, rather, is to analyze those anecdotes that illustrate what I believe to be four of the most important themes in Herodotus' work. A single point of resemblance, furthermore, joins these four themes: they are all antitheses or contradictions rather than single ideas. These anecdotes either present internal contradictions or absurdities, or they illustrate points of view that sharply contradict other anecdotes, offering in either case diametrically opposed points of view about each of four antitheses. Thus, as I will argue later, this very emphasis on contrariety is central to Herodotus' thought and to his intent in writing the *Histories.*

That Herodotus in general favors stories that illustrate the motif of "extreme opposites" seems obvious and has been taken for granted. But the phenomenon has never been closely studied because these are the exaggerated curiosities storytellers like to tell.[12] The stories that fall under this rubric examine extremes in nature or in human behavior or else they illustrate opposing conceptions of life. On the opposite sides of an African lake, we learn, live tribes that shave the opposite sides of their heads (4.180). If there are really Hyperboreans who live in the extreme North, Herodotus states he is also ready to believe in the existence of "Hypernotians" who dwell in the extreme South (4.36). When the Spartans defeat the Argives in battle, the former grow long hair in triumph, the latter cut theirs short in remorse (1.82). The ancient Lydians, to distract themselves from a grim famine, invent frivolous games and spend exactly half their time playing them. When the famine endures, half the Lydians emigrate to Italy, half stay behind (1.94). Timid animals are prolific, fierce animals bear few young (3.108). The Spartan king Ariston marries the most beautiful of women, who once was the ugliest of babies (6.61). Crocodiles are blind in the water but keenly sighted on land (2.68). Egyptian men urinate squatting, women standing up (2.35), and so forth.[13]

The most interesting of Herodotus' anecdotes that illustrate "extreme opposites," however, are those that present a contrast of ideas rather than just anthropological curiosities. Herodotus may hope to amuse the reader with the Padaeans, who eat their dead and even the seriously ill (who, Herodotus says, protest to their hungry relatives that they really are feeling better), whereas other Indian tribes eat no meat whatsoever (3.99). But when we hear of another pair of tribes, one that mourns the birth of a child and celebrates funerals, and another that does the opposite (5.4,7), we are dealing with antithetical views of the nature and value of human life. Xerxes demonstrates a similarly contrary attitude when he laughs with proud delight at the sight of his army but then only a moment later weeps as he reflects that all his men will be dead in a hundred years (7.45).[14] Closely allied with this type of story and equally curious is the phenomenon of opposite pairs of ideas or points of view illustrated in separate anecdotes or separate groups of anecdotes rather than in a single story. One group of anecdotes, for example, represents Themistocles as a wise general (e.g., 7.143; 8.83), whereas another shows him as a self-serving rascal (e.g., 8.75, 109). On some occasions Herodotus shows the gods generally being helpful and rewarding good conduct (1.31, 91; 8.13, 84; 9.65) but on others encouraging wickedness and increasing human suffering (1.32, 159; 2.133; 6.135; 9.93).

In some cases, as scholars have seen, Herodotus echoes the antithetical thinking of the sophists, pressed to its absurd extreme by Gorgias of Leontini and aptly parodied in A. E. Housman's "Fragment of a Greek Tragedy":

> And O my son, be, on the one hand, good,
> and do not, on the other hand, be bad.[15]

But sophistic influence cannot account for all the antitheses in Herodotus, nor is his literary style particularly antithetical.

If we look at this presentation of extreme opposites as a deliberate artistic choice rather than as proof of Herodotus' unrigorous thinking or failure to select consistent stories, we must accept a different author from the raconteur of naive charm encountered in the handbooks. Herodotus has always suffered more from his good reputation as a charming story-teller than from his bad reputation as a liar. The tendency has been to dismiss his "ideas" as clichés: "count no man happy till he dies," or "pride goeth before a fall." Even these clichés, it is alleged, Herodotus took secondhand, mostly from Attic tragedy.

One problem in arguing against this position is that one person's cliché is another's profound insight. Still, the simplicity of an idea does not and should not detract from its truth or worth. Many literary masterpieces, moreover, only elaborate a cliché. In the *Oresteia* Aeschylus takes a piece of proverbial wisdom, παθήματα μαθήματα, "once bitten, twice shy," rephrases it slightly, πάθεϊ μάθος, "through suffering, wisdom," and repeats it artfully to transform a cliché into a powerful statement of the human predicament.[16] Although in Herodotus the point of a single anecdote may appear to be a cliché, the cumulative effect of its repetition through the *Histories* results, as I hope to show, in new insight. Already, if we can see that Herodotus' anecdotal opposites are part of his art, we have accepted a new level of complexity in the *Histories*. Herodotus in these anecdotes refuses to say that life is a mean between extremes. He sees life, rather, as a series of extreme and even mutually exclusive opposites. Thus, Herodotus' view of his subject is supremely ironic, and his intent in writing is to make his readers share that view.

I believe that attentive readers of Herodotus have always intuitively sensed his irony and complexity of attitude about the events he describes. J. D. Denniston, for example, compared Herodotus' serio-comic tone to that of Mozart's music: on the surface lighthearted, but with "a note of profound sadness and pity sounded not seldom in his history."[17] My intent here is to write a book that will listen for and analyze this playful, Mozartean tone in the *Histories*. As a student I looked in vain for explication of this aspect of Herodotus' work in writings about him. A remark by a teacher I admired, the late Adam Parry, about Herodotus' "archaic smile" seemed and still seems to me to capture this conception of the historian. The term is derived from a stylistic trait of archaic Greek statues of young men and women of the "kouroi" type. The mouths have an upturn at the corners, and the faces consequently appear to be slightly smiling. Experts tell us that this is not a true smile but only the sculptor's effort to present all muscles, including those of the face, in a state of extreme tension.[18] Nevertheless, the viewer still sees a smile that suggests not only intelligence and insight but a playfully concealed secret. The onlooker feels drawn into a guessing game of the occasion for the smile. So, too, Herodotus' stories suggest a deeper meaning hidden behind their surface charm.

I have chosen to study four groups of anecdotes that illustrate the following antitheses: logic and accident, truth and fiction, nature and culture, discipline and freedom. No doubt there are others, and even these categories could be defined differently; but these four are central albeit neglected or misunderstood. By "logic" I mean the belief that the world functions according to understandable rules and that these rules are intel-

ligible to reasonable people. Herodotus has often been crit-
icized for *not* believing this, because so many of his explanations
for events are irrational, involving divine intervention or the
supernatural and unpredictable. I will attempt to show that
Herodotus is quite aware of reasonable explanations and in fact
engages in hyperrationalism on occasion, but that he does this
only to show that reason is just one possible explanation for
conduct. Against logic Herodotus ranges accidental events and
the irrational passions of human beings, often represented, as
we shall see, by the powerful symbol of the cruel and vengeful
queen.

Herodotus has also been blamed for not at all times
equally sharing Thucydides' passion for the truth of what actually happened, even telling tales that he admits are not true. I
will try to show, on the other hand, that Herodotus knows the
difference between truth and falsehood, but he attempts to
demonstrate, often in a playful way, that what actually happened—the truth—was trivial compared with an admittedly
fictional story that expresses a deeper kind of truth.

The conflict between nature and culture, I believe,
constitutes a central theme of the *Histories,* because Herodotus
describes the two opposed people, the Hellenes and the Persians, as men of nature and men of culture, or, as I shall call
them, noble savages and prosperous aggressors. But through
anecdotes, Herodotus argues that nature is not always superior
to culture, nor are all Greeks noble savages and all Persians
prosperous aggressors. Here I also hope to show how Herodotus uses the nature–culture antithesis to integrate the ethnographic portions of his text into the historical narrative.

Finally, in a chapter on discipline and freedom, I will
discuss undercurrents in the *Histories* of both criticism of the
free and undisciplined Greeks and admiration for the logical
and orderly Persians. Herodotus' heart lies with the former, but
his anecdotes show that, theoretically, the best system of government is the tyranny of a quasiphilosopher king. To the age-
old question, then, of whether Herodotus really is a "barbarian
lover" I will try to show that the truest answer lies tantalizingly
hidden behind his archaic smile.

1

Logic and Accident: Herodotus' "Archaeology" and the Motif of the "Clever, Vengeful Queen"

Macaulay assumes that one purpose of history is to derive principles from facts. Such a view, shared by Herodotus' successor, Thucydides, presumes that principles do underlie facts. Thucydides begins his *Peloponnesian Wars* with a statement of his principles (christened by scholars the "Archaeology"), a nineteen-chapter analysis of the past, designed to explain and illustrate his methodology. Thucydides writes that war is the ultimate test of political and military power, and a city, to succeed in war, must have money, walls, and ships. These three elements, then, are for him ἀξιόλογοι, "worthy of an account."[1]

Does Herodotus also believe that logic governs historical events, or does he describe only a series of unrelated accidents? I will argue that at the beginning of his book, Herodotus, like Thucydides, gives an explanation of his methodology, a comparable "Archaeology." Herodotus, however, does not explicitly explain his methods but uses a characteristic stylistic feature, the anecdote, to illustrate how he views the causes of events. Even more characteristically, I believe, Herodotus pre-

sents his "Archaeology" in the form of two, *contradictory* anecdotes, each illustrating an opposite set of principles for the
writing of history. Immediately after his introductory sentence,
in which he promises to give the αἰτία, "reason," why the
Hellenes and barbarians fought one another, he indeed gives a
reason, which he attributes to certain λόγιοι Περσέων, "Persian
authorities" (1.1).[2] These Persians allege that the Greeks have
wronged them since remote antiquity through the abductions
of the Asian princesses Europa and Medea. In the version in
which Herodotus tells these stories, logic, as we shall see, is the
dominant force that explains the action.

Herodotus then passes over this Persian *aitia,* which
he assigns to the remote and unverifiable world of myth and
fiction, and moves forward to the story of the accession of
Gyges to the throne of Lydia. Since Gyges is the ancestor of
Croesus, soon to be toppled by Cyrus, the ancestor of Xerxes,
and since Gyges has sent dedications to Delphi that Herodotus
has seen, Gyges clearly stands, for Herodotus, on the brink of
real history.[3] But Herodotus now tells a story about Gyges in
which accident and unpredictable passion, not logic, are the
theme; he then apparently accepts this story as fact. In these
two stories Herodotus reveals how he views history: events
may be logical and thus can be analyzed and explained by reason; or events may be accidental and unpredictable and cannot
be explained. These events simply happened. Thus the method
that Herodotus proposes to follow—if we take these two stories as an implied programmatic statement—is to include both
types of events, logical and accidental, because he finds both, to
borrow Thucydides' term, ἀξιόλογοι. We must first examine
these two stories of Herodotus' "Archaeology," the Persian
aitia and the tale of Gyges, and then consider how the book
Herodotus proceeds to write demonstrates the polarity of his
approach.

The story Herodotus puts first, and which I have
called the "Persian *aitia,*" is an alternate version of the Greek
epic tradition. Herodotus places it here to demonstrate one of
the two opposite ways history may be written. This story rationalizes the traditional accounts of Io, Europa, Medea, and

Helen, and presents them as if they were evidence cited by the Persians for the provocation they have received over the centuries from the Greeks. This passage has always puzzled scholars.[4] Why, for example, does Herodotus begin his book with the Persian *aitia* when he himself soon gives us to understand that he does not necessarily believe these events actually happened? He passes over the *aitia* with airy disdain: "Concerning these matters I am not going to say that they happened this way or perhaps some other way" (1.5.3). Scholars have never been able to agree, however, on exactly why Herodotus dismisses the *aitia* or even if he does.[5] Equally baffling is why Herodotus labels as "Persian" tales that are so patently Greek fifth-century rationalizations of native Hellenic myths.[6] The Persian stories are, in fact, not only Greek but, as I shall demonstrate, largely if not wholly Herodotean inventions. This story forms so obvious a counterpoint to the immediately succeeding story of Gyges that I think only an artistic purpose can explain its presence here.

Herodotus attributes to certain Persian "chroniclers" a story according to which Phoenician traders triggered the dispute between Hellenes and barbarians by carrying off Io from Argos (1.1); then, the Hellenes carried off Europa from Tyre in retribution (1.2.1). Next, the Greeks carried off Medea (1.2.2), and finally Alexander of Troy carried off Helen, precipitating the Trojan war (1.3) and provoking the Persians' scorn: "Up until now the Persians say it was a question of abductions back and forth, but from this point forward the Greeks were greatly worthy of blame, for they now attacked Asia with an army before the Asians attacked Europe" (1.4).

The chief and remarkable characteristic of the Persian *aitia* is rationalism, pushed to its absurd extreme. Herodotus here parodies not just myth but rationalism itself. He makes the very plausibility of these demythologized tales suspect, particularly through unspoken or barely hinted comparison with the poetic originals. First of all, Herodotus endows the Greek epic stories with an exact chronology. He joins together totally different and timeless myths in a logical and orderly chronological sequence of cause and effect never suggested by the originals. The removal of Io to Egypt leads certain Cretans to steal Europa from Tyre, which in turn inspires some Greeks to steal Medea from Colchis and then Alexander to steal Helen. Specific references to time lend an air of accuracy to the chronology. Herodotus tells us in the Io episode that the Phoenicians expose their wares on the beach for "five or six days" and then, later, that the rape of Helen occurs "in the second generation" after the voyage of the Argonauts. The same single cause, the abduction of a woman, with one theft leading inevitably to the next, links these events.

Although the stories are about the rape of women, what motivates these events is neither passion nor desire for revenge for outraged honor, but rather impersonal, economic causes. Herodotus thus rejects an emotional explanation in favor of a rational one. The first abduction, that of Io, takes place during—and as one purpose of—a Phoenician trading mission to Argos. Herodotus describes this stage in explicit detail. The Phoenicians expose their wares; then the Argives permit their womenfolk to examine the remaining trinkets. The Phoenicians, who, Herodotus shows us (2.54), have a habit of carrying off women and selling them abroad, have apparently been waiting for this opportunity, for they "give a signal" (1.1.4) and fall on the women. One of the women they carry off happens to be Io, the king's daughter, who, added to the Phoenicians' stock in trade, goes as chattel to Egypt. Only in the mischievously casual parenthesis, "not so the Greeks," οὐκ ὡς Ἕλληνες (1.2.1), does Herodotus refer to the familiar mythical version of Io's journey to Egypt: Zeus's guilty passion for her, the jealousy of Hera, Zeus's unguarded promise to Hera to give her anything she wants, and Io's subsequent transformation into a cow. Herodotus does not just suppress the supernatural elements of these stories, he insists emphatically on the unpoetic, unromantic commercial motives of his "Persian" version.

When in the next stage of events Europa has been carried off from Tyre, the "Persians" comment that this is now an "even exchange," ἴσα πρὸς ἴσα (1.2.1), implying that there is such a thing as an equal balance of trade between Phoenicia and Greece in the abduction of kings' daughters. We might compare this unsentimental attitude with the heroic world of Homer, where Achilles (*Il.* 9. 378–387) angrily rejects Agamemnon's offer of equal and even more than equal compensation for the theft of Briseis. In the Persian *aitia,* however, Herodotus affects the belief that there is such a thing as exactly equal compensation for wrongdoing and that, given equal compensation, men will not ask for more.

Herodotus also reduces the voyage of the Argonauts from the heroic and mythical to the plain and matter-of-fact. Herodotus' Argonauts, whom he prosaically describes as "Greeks," Ἕλληνας, do not seek magic talismans guarded by fire-breathing dragons, and they sail simply on "a long ship," μακρῇ νηί, not on the Argo, first of all ships. Herodotus ignores the fantastic details, never mentions Jason by name, and simply reports that "they" carried off the king's daughter, Medea, "after they had completed the other business on which they had come," διαπρηξαμένους καὶ τἆλλα τῶν εἵνεκεν ἀπίκατο (1.2.2). Once again the story illustrates a commercial theme. Similar, too, is Herodotus' Paris, who seizes Helen, not as Aphrodite's bribe, not from love or even lust, but with the cold calculation that he will not have to "pay" for her: "He heard of these things [the rape of Medea] and wanted to get himself a woman from Greece by abduction, believing that he surely would not have to pay compensation to the Greeks because they [the Argonauts] had not paid [for the abduction of Medea]" (1.3.1). Paris evidently feels that what is free for one should be free for all. Throughout this passage we can note an escalation in the economic motive behind the events. We begin with a simple question of bride-stealing and find by the end more and more mention of "compensation," which comes to displace in importance the abducted women for whose sake it is sought.

The narrative here proceeds swiftly, without drama or dialogue. No characters emerge as individuals, not even the famous women. Paris makes only a cameo appearance, and then not as a famous hero or lover but only as a type, a speculator who seizes the opportunity to get something for nothing. We hear human speech only indirectly in what pretend to be summaries of the hostile communiqués exchanged between the Trojans and Greeks before the Trojan War: "since the Greeks had returned neither compensation nor the girl, how could they . . . ?" The Trojans conclude with a marvelously cantankerous and cynical message: "They [the Trojans] said they thought it was scoundrels, to be sure, who carried off women, but only fools made a fuss about them and wise men paid them no mind whatsoever, for they would not be carried off if they did not want it" (1.4.2). The Trojan spokesmen's interpretation of events is crucial to the whole *aitia* passage, since it was Asians (Phoenicians) who started things by accidentally carrying off a king's daughter while on a trading mission. For these Trojans the business of life is business, and questions of honor involving women may be safely dismissed.

Herodotus calls into question the revisionist rationalism of writers like Hecataeus by ridiculing the crude beginnings of the historical method: the comparison of the reliability and plausibility of conflicting sources.[7] Herodotus acts as the impartial recorder of "what Persian chroniclers say," noting the agreement and disagreement of other sources and supplying his own conjectures to flesh out the evidence: "I believe these were probably Cretans." At the end of the Persian *aitia* Herodotus reports without comment an alternate "Phoenician" version of the story of Io, compressed into a single businesslike sentence: "The Phoenicians say she had intercourse with the [Phoenician] captain and, when she realized she was pregnant, became embarrassed to tell her parents and so sailed off with him willingly in order that her condition might escape detection" (1.5.2). The Phoenician version, though it is contrary to what the Persian chroniclers said and nakedly exculpatory, thus proves that the Trojan spokesmen were right about women who get themselves abducted.

Herodotus here, with playfully exaggerated seriousness, presents an utterly rationalized history: a series of unheroic events in which questions of fate, honor, and human values play no role. Even revenge Herodotus treats as an unemotional mechanism for adjusting grievances. Herodotus' Persian *aitia* constitutes a "good story," but not in the traditional sense. This passage achieves its witty effect precisely by suppressing all the piquant details the reader expects.

The next passage, which serves as a bridge between the Persian *aitia* and Gyges, signals an abrupt change of tone from the flat and dry style of the earlier passage and introduces a note of pathos, sadness even, for the loss of past greatness: "I shall go forward in my account, treating both small and great cities of men, for those which were great in ancient times have most of them become small, and those which in my day were great were formerly small. Because I know that human happiness never remains the same, I shall commemorate both alike" (1.5.3–4). The change in tone is Herodotus' clue to the reader that the next story will surely not, with the introduction of the motif of "human happiness," be a story in which emotions play no role.

The only other introduction Herodotus provides to the story of Gyges, the first real historical personage in the *Histories,* is a brief but dizzying genealogy of the Lydian royal house before the accession of Gyges (1.6–7). In this genealogy Herodotus skips backward and forward in time, giving neither a neat ring composition nor a straightforward and chronological movement from father to son. He mentions first Candaules' remote ancestor, Herakles, and then skips forward in time to Agron, a less remote ancestor, back again to Herakles, forward to Candaules again, and back finally to the primordial son of Atys, Lydus, who ruled long before Agron. Then Herodotus sums up in measured phrases: "They [the Heraclids] ruled twenty-two generations of men and five hundred five years, each son receiving the sovereignty from his father down to Candaules the son of Myrsus" (1.7.4). The next sentence begins with the brilliant story of Gyges, echoing the name of Candaules at the end of the genealogical proem: "Now this Candaules. . . ."

If Herodotus' earlier account of the Persian *aitia* is orderly and sober, his genealogy of Lydian kings is convoluted and chaotic. Herodotus' motives here, however, are artistic rather than scientific and objective, for he wants, first of all, to make a pointed contrast between the clear, organized sequence of *fictional* heroines and the chronologically confused list of *real* kings. He also wants to provide a suitably heroic and dramatic introduction for the story of Gyges and Candaules, two of the chief actors in the story he is about to tell. Candaules must come onstage freighted with his numerous and noble ancestors, for the usurper Gyges must seem to violate this unbroken dynastic tradition, a sin for which his descendant Croesus in the fifth generation must pay. Croesus, just as Candaules is the last Heraclid king of Lydia, will be the last Mermnad, indeed the last Lydian king of all. The story of Gyges thus begins in a mood of some fateful foreboding, for Herodotus portrays the shift in the kingship of Lydia from the Heraclids to the Mermnads as a momentous event.

This genealogical introduction, therefore, serves as a second clue to the reader that what Herodotus is about to say concerning Gyges and Candaules will differ in some striking way from what he has said about Io and Helen. The Gyges story, one of Herodotus' masterpieces, perfectly satisfies this expectation. Here transpires a brief but memorable drama of twisted desire, inscrutable fate, human weakness, and terrible vengeance, contrasting in every detail with Herodotus' cautiously plausible and undramatic retelling of the rationalized myths of the Persian *aitia*.

Although Herodotus writes about the Persian *aitia* in a flat narrative, he chooses vivid and dramatic dialogue for the Gyges story. The Persian *aitia* describes a series of events stretching over many generations, arranged in exact chronological sequence, and unified by the same single, secular cause and effect. The Gyges story, on the other hand, which takes place essentially within a single night and morning, sets out no clear cause and effect but only hints darkly at inscrutable fate and divine punishment. The action of the Persian *aitia* takes place all over the Mediterranean basin, whereas in the Gyges story a single palace bedroom suffices as a stage. The men and women in the Persian *aitia* are mere pawns before blind chance and the one-dimensional and predictable motivations that drive them. In the Gyges story, however, we meet in dramatic confrontation the unpredictable passions of three individuals who are painfully human. Herodotus here replaces the sober, impersonal economic calculation of the faceless barbarians and Greeks in the Persian *aitia* with personal and passionate revenge spurred by outraged honor. In sum, whereas the keynote of the Persian *aitia* is reason, the dominant theme in the story of Gyges is passion.

Yet we also possess other versions of the Gyges story that suggest these events might have been presented in a more rational and plausible way. Other sources tell us that the change in the Lydian dynasty took place when the king was murdered and the murderer married his queen and took over his kingdom. This is the basic story, but Herodotus does not, as do other sources, attribute the fall of one king and the rise of another to the personal ambitions of the successor, the logical human motivation provided by power, wealth, or sex. Historical evidence including Persian inscriptions, for example, presents the "real" Gyges as the scion of a competing Lydian royal house who seized power from Candaules in a relatively bloodless palace coup, in which, however, Candaules perished.[8] Nothing could be more realistic than the motive of political opportunism suggested by this historical record.

Plato, writing perhaps fifty years after Herodotus, records a different story of Gyges, but one that also attributes Gyges' rise to predictable and understandable human motives.[9] Here Gyges is not a royal usurper but a simple shepherd who discovers a magic ring that will make him invisible whenever he turns its signet inward. He immediately uses the ring to secure sex and power. He murders the king—we are not told how—marries the queen, and becomes king of Lydia. The magic ring and rags-to-riches motif argue this to be a folktale of great antiquity, essentially earlier than Herodotus and scarcely historical. Nevertheless, the motivation of Plato's Gyges is plausible. Magic only gives him the opportunity to act out the most basic, if selfish, human desires. In yet another surely fictional but essentially realistic version of the Gyges story, Gyges attempts to rape the wife and then kills the king in order to forestall vengeance.[10]

In his version of the Gyges story, however, Herodotus rejects reasonable motives for dramatic and bizarre ones. Even if Herodotus were aware of none of the other Gyges traditions known to us, the story he gives us hardly describes the most plausible route by which the murderer of a king may become king in his stead. Herodotus' Gyges has no ambitions, plausible or otherwise. Rather, it is the queen, of no account in the other versions, who bullies Gyges into killing his master to satisfy her private lust for revenge. But the precipitating force in the story is the most bizarre of all: a husband's wish to have another man see his wife naked. Herodotus narrates this story, the first event in real history, in a vivid style that shuns the scientific remoteness of the Persian *aitia*. Herodotus rejects the device of telling the story as a report of what someone says happened or as a tale that may or may not be true. He never thereafter questions the version he gives or suggests the existence of alternatives.[11] His Gyges tale begins with the directness and immediacy of a folktale: "Now this Candaules was smitten by a passion for his own wife, and in his passion he believed her to be the most beautiful of all women." The vivid ἠράσθη, "was smitten by a passion" (1.8.1), alerts us to a peculiar situation, for it seems unlikely that a sovereign monarch should be unable to satisfy his passion for his wife.[12] The next clause, however, makes clear what is even more peculiar: this passion cannot be satisfied by normal sexual means. His obsession, rather, fixes on his wife's physical appearance and on compelling others to share his admiration for her beauty: "His belief in her beauty had the following result. He had a certain spear bearer he particularly liked, Gyges the son of Daskylus, and he therefore not only confided in this Gyges about important affairs but was always praising to the skies to him his wife's beauty" (1.8.1). These words carry on the impression of an abnormal sexuality, for Candaules' admiration is only for his wife's "appearance," εἶδος. Herodotus also hints that Candaules has been neglecting affairs of state in his infatuation and relying overmuch on Gyges.

The story continues: "After some time had passed, for it was necessary for Candaules to end ill . . ." (1.8.2). Here, in the phrase "after some time," and elsewhere in the story ("when it was time for sleep" [1.10.1], "when morning came" [1.11.1]), Herodotus indicates time in a general and unspecific way much in the style of a folktale. Here, in other words, he eschews the precise chronology of the Persian *aitia*. In this story it is "necessary" for Candaules to die, for in such tales some characters are always obscurely marked for destruction. Fate and the gods play a role, too, though not a clear one, for Candaules' own intransigent persistence in folly also contributes to the inevitability of his demise. Through his own witlessness he had an irresistible impulse to do wrong. Herodotus' use of similar terminology for "had to end badly" in other stories indicates the often close compliance of individual disposition and divine plan.[13]

The specific wrong that Candaules is compelled or feels compelled to do is to violate the law or customs of the Lydians, their *nomos*, which guards the modesty of both men and women, Herodotus says (1.10.3), from prying eyes. Gyges indeed quite properly seeks to escape from Candaules' dreadful demands by an appeal to *nomos:* "Do not require of me actions which are contrary to law," ἀνόμων (1.8.4). Once the deed is done and discovered, Candaules' wife confronts Gyges with "acts contrary to law," οὐ νομιζόμενα (1.11.3).[14]

The subjects of fate and guilt and the violation of *nomos* introduced in this story contrast with the Persian *aitia* where neither individual human will and guilt nor divine direction played a role. It was a desire for profit, we recall, and not fate that brought the Phoenician traders to Argos on the occasion when they seized Io. We can recall also that the Persian spokesmen specifically rejected the idea that men guilty of violations against honor or crimes against propriety were worth punishing. The very motives Herodotus has rejected or expunged from the Persian account of Greek epic he accepts in the story of Gyges.

The style of the Gyges story further emphasizes its contrast with the Persian *aitia*. In the story of Gyges Herodotus skillfully uses the direct speech and dialogue he kept out of the Persian *aitia*. Herodotus uses conversation to bring life and individuality to his three speakers, who thus differ strikingly from the faceless characters of the Persian *aitia*. Herodotus begins by contrasting the crazed intensity of Candaules with the cringing, terrified response of Gyges:

> "Gyges, I don't think you believe me when I tell you about my wife's looks [εἶδος, again]. Since men's ears are harder to convince than their eyes, you must find a way to see her naked." Gyges answered by crying out loudly and saying: "Master! What have you said! An unhealthy idea, asking me to look at my mistress naked! When a woman takes off her clothes, she takes off her respectability. Men of old found out the best ways, and from these ways we must learn. One of these is: 'Let each man look upon his own.' I do believe you when you say she is the most beautiful of women." (1.8.2–4)[15]

Herodotus delays the titillating key word in Candaules' speech, "find a way to see her *naked*," γυμνήν, till the end and to the end of Gyges' first sentence of reply: ". . . to look at my mistress *naked!*" γυμνήν. This parallelism allows us to hear the different tones of voice in which master and servant pronounce the same word, Candaules with unhealthy relish, Gyges with nervous alarm. Gyges echoes Candaules' phraseology in other respects as well. This repetition, both a feature of archaic style and a normal tendency in any conversation, is here exaggerated by the spear bearer's tactful attempts to humor yet dissuade his deranged master. Gyges repeats not just γυμνήν, *naked,* but also Candaules' colorful word for "see," θεήσεαι . . . θεήσασ- θαι, and his plaintive "I *do* believe you" answers Candaules' suspicious "I don't think that you believe me." Gyges answers Candaules' single proverb about eyes and ears with two proverbs. Moreover, Gyges gives to the word "look" in "look to his own" a special application to his own case, the "looking" Candaules wants him to do.

> "Take courage, Gyges. Do not be afraid of me that I am proposing this to test you or afraid of my wife that some harm might come to you through her. First, I shall contrive that she will not know she has been seen by you. I shall station you in the room in which we sleep, behind the open door. After me, my wife will

come to bed. There is a chair close to the entrance. On it she will place each of her garments one by one as she takes them off, and she will enable you to look at her with great leisure. But when she walks from the chair to the bed, make sure she does not see you going out through the doors." (1.9.1–3)

Candaules' words here, particularly the lavish description of the—apparently nightly—slow striptease, complete Herodotus' portrait of Candaules' obsession. We also note that the specific physical setting of the story contrasts sharply with that of the Persian *aitia,* where events took place against an anonymous broad landscape or in no particular setting at all. Here in the Gyges story, we enter an intimate, carefully imagined interior space, a particular bedroom furnished with a particular chair. This chair, precisely because it is not crucial to the story and has no symbolic meaning, adds a vivid realistic touch.

> Now Gyges, since he could not escape, gave in. Candaules, when he decided it was time for bed, led Gyges to the room. Immediately afterwards came his wife. As she came in and took off her clothes, Gyges looked at her. Then as the wife turned her back to go toward the bed, he silently crept out. But the woman caught sight of him as he went out. Now realizing that the deed was her husband's, she did not cry out that she had been shamed, nor even let on that she knew, because she was planning her vengeance on Candaules. . . . For the time being she revealed nothing and remained calm. (1.10.1–11.1)

Although the famous women of the Persian *aitia* were ciphers apart from their names, Candaules' wife, though unnamed, dominates the scene. She is not only beautiful but, as we now learn, clever. Seeing Gyges in her bedroom, she does not unthinkingly jump to the most obvious conclusion, that Gyges has either turned assassin in a palace coup or is a peeping Tom in his own right. In either case she ought to denounce the intruder instantly to Candaules.[16] But she knows her husband so well that she immediately realizes why Gyges is there and who is responsible. A papyrus fragment of a "Gyges tragedy" (whether earlier or later than Herodotus does not matter for our purposes here) has the wife realize that Candaules is responsible only when she notices that his eyes are open—that he, too, sees Gyges and is untroubled by his presence in the bedroom.[17] The comparison with Herodotus is instructive, for Herodotus wants to call attention to the wife's superior intelligence by having her guess the truth of the situation without any specific clue. Compare also in Herodotus the wife's understanding of Candaules with his ignorance of her. His knowledge of her is superficial, for he cannot see beyond her appearance. Candaules does not know that he is married to a formidable woman who may become a dangerous adversary if his plan of exhibiting her to Gyges goes awry.[18]

Candaules' wife's self-control matches her intelligence, for she suppresses any reaction: "She did not cry out," οὔτε ἀνέβωσε (1.10.2). Contrast the wife's firmness with the cowardice of Gyges in his earlier conversation with Candaules when the king's favorite "cried out loudly," μέγα ἀμβώσας (1.8.2), in almost feminine alarm at the mere *idea* of seeing his mistress naked. Once again, the repetition of a crucial word reveals Herodotus' art.

The care with which the wife plans her revenge reveals her perspicacity even more:

> As soon as it was day she called those of the household who were most faithful to her, and, making them ready, summoned Gyges. He, not suspecting she knew anything of what had happened, came at her call, for he was accustomed to come when the queen called. When Gyges arrived, the queen spoke to him as follows: "Now you have two routes to follow, and I give you the choice of which you want to take. Either kill Candaules and have me and the sovereignty over the Lydians or else you must die here and now so that you may never again, through slavishly obeying Candaules, see what you should not. Either the man who planned this must die or you who saw me naked and did what is contrary to our customs." Gyges was for a while dumbfounded by what she had said. (1.11.1–3)

Unlike Candaules, his wife takes careful precautions before committing herself to action. She readies allies within the household, and it is significant both that she has allies and that Candaules took no such precautions before scheming to violate her privacy. Then she confronts Gyges, whom she understands perfectly. She knows Gyges as a man of good intention but a weakling, easily frightened and set on a course of action that, upon reflection, he could and should avoid. No wonder Candaules earlier had to urge him: "Take courage, Gyges!" But the reader may well share Gyges' shock at the wife's daring and in particular at the terrible finality of the revenge she plans. Nothing but the death penalty will do, nor will she give the defendant any chance to plead his case. Her smoldering, dramatically delayed, and carefully planned revenge brings upon Candaules punishment out of all proportion to his crime.

> Gyges then begged her not to compel him by force to make a choice like this. He did not, however, persuade her. Rather, he saw there was an absolute power forcing him either to kill his master or be killed by others. He chose survival. Now he questioned her, asking: "Since you force me, unwilling though I am, to kill my master, come, I will listen. How shall we lay hands on him?" She answered, saying: "The attack will be in the same spot where he showed me to you naked. We will set on him when he is asleep." When they had arranged the plan and night had fallen—since Gyges was not free and had no escape, for either he or Candaules had to die—he followed the woman into her room. She gave him a dagger and hid him behind that same door. Afterwards, when Candaules had retired, Gyges slipped out, killed him, and took possession of both his wife and his kingdom. (1.11.3–1.12.2)

Gyges, unaware that his attempt to escape from the bedroom unnoticed has been unsuccessful and oblivious to the trap laid for him, now incautiously places himself in his mistress's power. He cannot now escape, though he makes a pitiful attempt to do so. He must choose between his own death and his master's. His choice in Herodotus' eyes, however, is not so much between death and life as between the honor of noble self-sacrifice and the dishonor of betraying the fealty he owes his master. What he ought to do is clear. Elsewhere in his book Herodotus describes with approval the actions of men like

Arion, Prexaspes, and Boges who face death, as Gyges does, but who then go to meet it bravely and even with flair.[19] Gyges is not only cowardly, foolish, and clumsy (did his foot scrape on the threshold of that door?), he is also remarkably passive. Once he has made the choice of betraying Candaules, he turns automatically to the wife for specific instructions: "How shall we lay hands upon him?" He has no plan himself and puts himself blindly in her hands. She must even supply him with the dagger to do the deed.

The *Histories* thus begins with two stories illustrating two alternative conceptions of historical causation. In the first Herodotus rejects all irrational explanations; in the second he accepts them. If these two anecdotes are programmatic for the *Histories,* we need now to examine how Herodotus uses the methodologies illustrated by these anecdotes throughout his book. We will look first at the method of writing history illustrated by the Persian *aitia:* a description of a logical series of events in which reason rules over passion. If we look at the broad outlines of the *Histories,* we find many other examples. Book One, whose subject is the rise of the Persian empire under Cyrus, describes the expansionism that leads the Persians into inevitable conflict with their neighbors. Herodotus tells how the Persians first absorb the Lydian empire of Croesus (who has already conquered some of the Greek cities of Asia Minor), then turn south against Egypt and Ethiopia, then north against the Scythians, and finally west against the Greeks. Herodotus further explains how a difference in ideology between the free Hellenic societies and the totalitarian Persian empire led to a revolt by the Ionian Greek cities. This revolt in turn provoked first Darius and then Xerxes to take vengeance on the mainland Greeks (and especially Athens) for their support of the rebels. In outline, then, Herodotus' *Histories* shares with the Persian *aitia* a clear direction and an orderly series of events.

A similar order characterizes Herodotus' physical universe, particularly in the ethnographic sections describing the flora and fauna of remote areas and the customs of remote peoples. Here, as I noted in the Introduction, we find a world of balances and polarities. Some phenomena are equally distributed over the earth, but where there are concentrations or absences, Herodotus explains these distortions as if they were part of a symmetrical scheme. Thus lions are not found everywhere in Europe because the entire world's supply of them is concentrated between the Nestos and Acheloos rivers (7.126). Although lions may be clustered near the world's center, other occurrences, both in nature generally and in human behavior, balance one another at opposite points of the compass. So, for example, the Scythians in the north and the Egyptians in the south have customs that are in some cases strikingly similar, in others strikingly dissimilar. Both shun foreign customs (2.79.1, 91.1; 4.76.1), but the Scythians consider themselves the youngest of cultures (4.5.1); the Egyptians call themselves the oldest (2.2.1). Scythia has many rivers (4.82), Egypt only one (4.47.1), and so forth, a mechanically balanced world whose order is pushed to the extremes demonstrated by the Persian *aitia*.[20] And yet, as with the Persian *aitia,* the more we examine this orderliness the more absurd and remote it seems from human experience. When Herodotus tells about a people living beyond the Scythians, all of whose men and women are bald from birth (φαλακροὶ ἐκ γενεῆς γινόμενοι), the reader can easily complete the sentence with the appropriate polar phenomenon, namely, that these men and women all have long beards (καὶ γένεια ἔχοντες μεγάλα [4.23.2]). Such passages often read like parodies of some of the dark polar maxims of Heracleitus. Herodotus may well betray his ironical attitude to such rationalizations when, in a rare explicit statement of opinion, he says: "I laugh when I contemplate the work of many geographers . . . who make Asia the same size as Europe" (4.36).[21]

We find the same echo of the Persian *aitia* when we turn from content to method. As we have seen, in the *aitia* passage Herodotus strips away from myth all its irrational elements of love, passion, and revenge until all that is left is a dry document describing only quasi-commercial, quasi-legal transactions. Herodotus applies the same rationalist logic to many stories and particularly to details within a story. He doubts, for example, that the infant Cyrus was suckled by a wolf, saying it was more likely he was nursed by a shepherd's wife whose name meant "she-wolf" (1.122). Similarly when Herodotus describes how Psammetichus isolates some children from human contact in order to discover in what language they will utter their first words, the historian doubts that this Egyptian king actually cut out the tongues of the women assigned to care for the babies (2.2.5).[22] In the Persian *aitia* there lies in the background a myth so well known (even though Herodotus scarcely mentions that another version of the stories of Helen and Io exists) that the reader recognizes the tension between the rational and the irrational alternatives. In such stories as those of Cyrus and Psammetichus, however (perhaps because they are less well known), Herodotus gives two versions or, typically, doubts or rationalizes a detail in the story but does not reject the rest of the tale.[23] In this way, just as in the Persian *aitia*, Herodotus puts the irrational in direct conflict with the rational. A wolf may not have suckled Cyrus, it seems, but there is no doubt he shared with Herakles, Oedipus, and others a childhood rich in other folktale motifs. Nor does Herodotus doubt that Psammetichus did cloister children or that their first word was "bekos," the Phrygian word for bread.

Herodotus' recurrent but apparently inconsistent "skepticism" forms a controversial topic to which I will return in the next chapter, where I will try to show its role in the antithesis between truth and fiction. One other kind of Herodotean rationalism deserves treatment here: his references to surviving monuments to show by incontrovertible physical proof that the events commemorated by monuments actually occurred. Conversely, stories that have left no physical traces may be rejected as myths.[24] Thus Herodotus looks for the buildings, tombs, dedications, inscriptions, and other physical traces that show that the men who left them behind once lived and are not figments of poetic imagination. He touches on this particular rationalizing element in the *Histories* in the "small and great cities of men" passage, which introduces the story of Gyges. It is appropriate that Herodotus should mention physical remains of ancient cities (some now in ruins that were once great) at just this point, for the presence of physical testimonia is just what distinguishes the historical Gyges from the doubtful world of Greek myth in the Persian *aitia*. Herodotus closes his account of Gyges with a catalogue of the dedications the new Lydian king sent to Delphi. Thus Gyges, and after him Croesus, are real men because they sent dedications to Delphi that Herodotus himself has seen and studied, whereas Europa and Io left no tangible memorials of themselves. Later in the *Histories*, too, Herodotus uses visible evidence to distinguish the remote and uncertain from recent true history.[25] The Persian sack of Athens, for example, is no dim legend for Herodotus because the signs of the fire on the Acropolis are still visible (5.77.3) and the Thracians still leave untilled the route of Xerxes' march through their country (7.115). Nevertheless, the distinction that Herodotus makes between the Persian *aitia* and the Gyges story is more one of narrative style than one of strict chronological separation between myth and history, for the writer later (2.118) does accept the Trojan war as a real event, a judgment based, as we might expect, on archaeological remains in Egypt (2.112).

But once again we see that the writer brings the worlds of reason and passion into direct conflict for, as in the case of Gyges, Herodotus throughout the *Histories* tells stories about the emotional or irrational behavior of men and women whose reality he has confirmed by concrete evidence. Cheops' pyramid, for example, is proof of the pharaoh's having prostituted his daughter to provide funds for the building's construction, and she too builds with her tips a pyramid at whose size Herodotus exclaims (2.124–126). No doubt what appeals to Herodotus about this story is that it presents a captivating contrast between a gigantic, awe-inspiring monument and the far-fetched tale of human passion it confirms. With similar ironic pleasure, perhaps, Herodotus notes that the class of prostitutes made the largest contribution to Alyattes' impressive tomb (1.93).

The Gyges anecdote sets the stage for a dramatic style of writing, opposite from that of the Persian *aitia*. We can of course easily find many places in the *Histories* where human passions motivate events, but the Gyges story introduces two major motifs—the "violation of *nomos*" and the "clever, vengeful queen"—that Herodotus repeats again and again. The importance of the *nomos* motif for the *Histories,* both νόμος, "custom" and νομός, "region," is well known. After Gyges we meet a series of barbarian kings and one Athenian, Miltiades (6.134–135), who violate *nomos* by overstepping physical or moral boundaries, just as Candaules violates the customs of the Lydians by exhibiting his wife naked. Herodotus' disapproval is clear and generally recognized, as Cambyses profanes Egyptian religion by stabbing the Apis bull (3.30), or Xerxes profanes nature by digging a canal through the Athos peninsula (7.24). Our particular interest here, however, is to show that the contrast between the Gyges story and the Persian *aitia* is between logic and accident. For this contrast the motif of the "clever, vengeful queen" is crucial. This motif, not generally recognized and never thoroughly studied, appears often, I believe, and is more important for understanding the *Histories* than the "violation of *nomos.*"

The constituent elements in this motif are the woman's cleverness, the personal or family motive for her revenge, the intricacy of her planning—often over a period of time—and the horrible and usually bloody nature of the revenge itself, which outstrips in ferocity the degree of insult that provoked it. Another significant element in the motif (though more evident in some stories than in others) is the moral ambivalence of the vengeful female figure: Candaules' wife is both splendid and dreadful in her anger. Herodotus neither wholly applauds her nor condemns her.

After Candaules' wife, we next meet this clever, vengeful woman in the person of Tomyris, the Massagete queen who defeats Cyrus in battle and then dips his severed head in a bucket of blood, bidding him drink his fill (1.205–215). Tomyris' desire for revenge is prompted not just by an earlier defeat but by the death of her son, whom Cyrus killed after first fuddling the boy's wits with the wine from a Persian banquet. We note the similarity of the exact specificity of Tomyris' revenge—she intends, she says, to give Cyrus his fill of blood just as he gave her son his fill of wine (1.212, 214.5)—with that of Candaules' wife, who wanted her husband killed "in the same place" where she suffered her insult. Similar to Tomyris (though her vengeance is more justified) is the Egyptian queen Nitocris, who punishes those responsible for the death of her brother by inviting them to a feast (2.100) in an elaborate underground chamber that she floods at the height of the dinner. A subsidiary theme—"the fatal banquet," fatal to Tomyris' son as it is to Nitocris' enemies—also links these two stories.[26] Nitocris then avoids retribution by committing suicide in a "brave gesture" that recalls the nobility of Arion and Prexaspes and thus illustrates the most positive moral side of the "clever, vengeful woman." This Egyptian Nitocris also recalls the Babylonian Nitocris. Though this queen's revenge is not bloody, she at least has the last laugh on Cyrus, even years after her death, and so contrives the most delayed revenge of any of these clever women. A misleading inscription on her tomb leads the Persian king to rifle it in the hopes of treasure, but he finds only the queen's desiccated corpse and a vindictive note from her (1.187).

Decidedly bloody is the revenge of Pheretima (4.165, 202), who, like Tomyris, punishes those responsible for the death of her son. She impales the men "in a circle" around the walls of Barcae, cuts off the breasts of their wives, and arranges these around the bodies of the husbands in a ghoulish display. Later, Herodotus says that the gods punish Pheretima's "excessive" revenge with a horrible, fatal disease (4.205), making her the most clearly despicable vengeful queen as the Egyptian Nitocris was the most admirable. Finally, on virtually the last page of the *Histories,* Herodotus tells a story that forms a companion piece to the story of Gyges at the book's beginning: "the revenge of Amestris" (9.108–112).[27] This jealous queen tricks the foolish Xerxes into putting into her power a woman whose daughter Xerxes has made his concubine. Curiously, Amestris holds the mother responsible for Xerxes' affair with the daughter. The besotted Xerxes seals the daughter's fate when he imprudently offers to grant her any wish she may have. She asks for a special cloak that was a present to him from Amestris. He begs her to ask any other favor except this one, but she persists and he gives in, and in so doing recalls for us the foolish pliancy of Gyges. The cloak betrays the affair to Amestris, who then at Xerxes' birthday feast, at which anyone may ask and receive a favor of the king, asks for power over the mother of Xerxes' concubine. Xerxes attempts unsuccessfully to deflect Amestris from her purpose. His pleas remind us again of Gyges. But Amestris will not yield and has the offending woman's breasts cut off and her tongue and lips cut off and thrown to the dogs, an egregious revenge, particularly considering this is the concubine's mother and not the girl herself. Her bloodthirstiness recalls both Tomyris and Pheretima as well as Candaules' wife. The Amestris story also raises twice over the significant folktale motif of the "fatal promise" of Xerxes, first to his lover and then to his wife (cf. 6.62).

The dominant motif of the Gyges story, however, is the wife's delayed, carefully planned and excessive revenge. We find this motif not just in other anecdotes in the *Histories* but in the finale of Herodotus' historical narrative as well.[28] Candaules' wife seeks a revenge that is out of proportion to the insult she has received from Candaules. Herodotus portrays the expedition of Xerxes against Greece as a similar act of excessive vengeance but on a grandiose scale. Candaules' wife spends but a single night in plotting her revenge, but Xerxes takes four full years to muster his forces (7.20, cf. 7.1). Xerxes' provocations were substantial—the Ionian revolt and his father's failure at Marathon—but not on the same scale as the stupendous expedition he mounts to requite them.

Yet Xerxes fails in the end to exact vengeance, whereas Candaules' wife succeeded. Herodotus' explanation lies in another subsidiary theme of the "clever, vengeful woman" motif: the triumph of this clever woman over a stupid man. We have seen how helpless Candaules and Gyges are against the wife's intelligence. The Xerxes of the Amestris story is no different. In Herodotus, therefore, we associate acts of delayed but extravagant vengeance with women and we expect success. Xerxes' vengeance fails because the intelligence—or rather the stupidity—that guides it is male instead of female. Herodotus repeatedly calls attention to Xerxes' foolishness and lack of foresight. Though Xerxes' preparations lack nothing in terms of physical extravagance and even magnificence, he fails, for example, to realize—despite specific warnings (7.10)—that the very size of his army may present difficulties. So just as Candaules' wife is but one among many "clever, vengeful women who always succeed," Candaules and Xerxes are but two of many "foolish men who always fail" (Croesus and Darius, for example). A bizarre prodigy, the birth of a hermaphrodite foal with male sexual organs over the female, attends Xerxes' march into Greece (7.57).[29] Given the motifs of female success and male failure, this omen darkly portends the slimness of Xerxes' chances. Then at Salamis, Artemisia—a Persian ally—cleverly escapes enemy pursuit by sinking a Persian ship and thus impresses the uncomprehending Xerxes, who complains that his men have become women and his women men (8.88). He ought, more specifically, to encourage his men to *think* like women—in fact, more like all those wily women who play such an important symbolic role in the *Histories*.

Scenes in which women play a dominant role are not confined to Herodotus' accounts of the exotic East with its perfumed harems. For example, Herodotus represents as an important passage in early Athenian history and another violation of *nomos* the decision of Pisistratus to have only unnatural—and therefore infertile—intercourse with the daughter of Megacles (1.61.1). In a single sentence Herodotus implies a whole series of embarrassing, intimate scenes: "She [the daughter of Megacles] kept silent about this [her husband's treatment of her], but then, either because she was questioned about it or not, she told her mother and the mother then told her husband" (1.61.2).

Nor would it be correct to take the motif of the "clever, vengeful woman" literally or as a reflection of the private feelings of the writer about real women. The myth of feminine evil is pervasive in all cultures, particularly so in Greek society, and Herodotus cannot wholly escape the prejudices of his own culture.[30] What shows, however, that Herodotus' vengeful queens are symbolic of passion, and that historical events are accidental and not expressive of the writer's specific fears, is that even in passages not involving women, we find Herodotus opting for the irrational explanation. Herodotus shows, for example, that the Persian defeat at Marathon did not lead inevitably to Salamis ten years later, in the same way as in the Persian *aitia* the voyage of the Argonauts led inevitably two generations later to the Trojan war. The chain of events that started with the fall of Croesus, in fact, breaks down by the time of Darius.

A boil on the breast of Darius' wife, Atossa, gives a homesick Greek doctor the opportunity to plant in Darius' mind the idea of attacking Greece (3.133), but the initial scouting mission comes to nothing. The Ionian revolt against the Persian empire may be plausible on ideological grounds as the effective cause of the battle of Marathon, but Herodotus portrays this revolt as primarily the result of the selfish plotting of the Greek adventurer, Histiaeus. Even if we set aside the passages where Herodotus strongly hints at the intercession of a deity, many unpredictable and irrational events play a role in the fall of Croesus, the rise of Cyrus, and Xerxes' invasion. A soldier's helmet, for example, rolls accidentally down a cliff and demonstrates that Sardis is not impregnable (1.84). A horse has to be coaxed into neighing at the proper moment to confirm Darius as the king of Persia (3.87), and an unrelated war with Aegina has to prompt the Athenians to equip a navy fit later to oppose the Persians (7.144).

Furthermore, Xerxes was initially ill-disposed toward taking vengeance on the Greeks. Only a series of dreams at first lures Xerxes to attack Greece and then actually threatens him if he does not (7.12ff). Artabanus provides a reasonable explanation of these dreams: they are merely thoughts that the dreamer has had during the day, and which the mind turns over at random in sleep. Artabanus specifically rejects the idea that these are supernatural dreams sent by the gods and are not rationally explicable: οὐδε ταῦτα . . . θεῖα (7.16β2). It was thus "necessary" for Xerxes to attack Greece for the same inscrutable nexus of human and divine reasons that determined it was "necessary" for Candaules to end ill.

Furthermore, evidence for such θεῖα τῶν πραγμάτων (9.100.2) does not peter out toward the end of the *Histories* as we might expect—as the narrative approaches a presumably more "historical" period. Supernatural omens, in fact, occur at regular intervals as Herodotus approaches his conclusion: an eclipse (7.37), a bolt of lightning (7.42), holy armor miraculously moved at Delphi (8.37), the regrowth of Erechtheus' olive (8.55), ghostly Bacchic choirs heard on the Thriasian plain (8.65), a phantom female warrior (8.84), a magic ship (8.94), and a sudden riptide (8.129).

I hope I have shown, then, that the *Histories* begins with two consciously contrasted stories that, together, function as a program for the whole work. These stories contrast logic and accident as the dominant forces in history. Moreover, as we have seen, each of these stories contains an internal contrast or contradiction. Through exaggeration in the Persian *aitia* Herodotus criticizes rationalism even as he relentlessly applies it to the Greek traditions about the past. Similarly, the Gyges story presents the irrationalism of personal motivation in a form so extreme as to challenge the reader's credulity and make one think perhaps once again with favor on the cool reason of the Persian *aitia*. The relation between the two stories has been overlooked, perhaps because they are so dissimilar in approach and content. But I believe dissimilarity, dissonance, and contradiction are essential features of the *Histories*.

In general, those critics who value Herodotus as a serious historian have concentrated their attentions on portions of the narrative where logic predominates, and they pass over in silence or dismiss the "good stories" of the *Histories*. Scholars with a less high opinion of Herodotus and whose intent is to characterize him as more storyteller than historian focus on the many passages where Herodotus attributes a crisis or its resolution to passion. By looking at both reason and passion and the conflict between the two as typical Herodotean explanations of human behavior and as characteristic of his style as a historian, I hope I have shown him to be more knowing than naive. If our feeling at the end of the *Histories* is that accident has outweighed logic as an explanation for historical events, Herodotus may be reacting negatively to the growing rationalism of his own age. His smile may be archaic, but it is deliberately so. Today in a nuclear age we are perhaps able to appreciate the wisdom of Herodotus' skepticism about the application of science to human behavior better than nineteenth-century critics of Herodotus who seized too fervently upon logic as the key to history.

2

Truth and Fiction:
ΨΕΥΔΕΑ ΠΟΛΛΑ ΕΤΥΜΟΙΣΙΝ ΟΜΟΙΑ

Thucydides strongly censures, at the beginning of his book, the uncritical attitude of his predecessors and contemporaries with regard to the truth (1.20.1, 20.3) and promises that he himself will get as close to the facts as possible (1.21.1). Even Herodotus' predecessor Hecataeus starts with a criticism of the "foolish" (*geloia*) stories of others and the anouncement that he will write "what I think is true" (ὥς μοι δοκεῖ ἀληθέα εἶναι [F-1]), although we may not think highly of the criteria by which Hecataeus sifts truth from fiction: a crude, reductive rationalism that assigns to the king Aegyptus considerably less than the canonical fifty sons but accepts this mythical king as a real person. Nevertheless, Hecataeus at least tries to extract (from the shadowy world of myth) a plausible account of what actually happened. Thucydides follows directly in the footsteps of Hecataeus by generally accepting the testimony of epic as a basis of historical research. Thucydides believes that an Argive king, Agamemnon, led forces against Troy—although his powerful position in Greece, and not any romantic suitors' oath to guard the purity of Helen's marriage, enabled him to do so (1.9.1). Similarly, there really did exist even before Agamemnon a Cretan king named Minos, whose powerful navy was the basis of his supremacy (1.4).

Although Herodotus does, just like Hecataeus and Thucydides, try to distinguish between truth and fiction, his conclusions appear contrary to common sense. He proposes a chronological line of demarcation between myth and history, namely, the reign of Gyges. Herodotus regards most prior events as fictitious, most subsequent events as true. Thus, as we have seen, Herodotus, more than Thucydides, criticizes the details of the Trojan war offered by Homer. He also consigns Minos, Thucydides' first admiral, to the world of myth, accepting instead the Samian Polycrates as the first "man of whom we really know," πρῶτος τῶν ἡμεῖς ἴδμεν (3.122), who ruled the sea.

But, on the other hand, Herodotus does not ever state at the beginning of his book or anywhere else that he will tell only the truth about the past, for the father of history does not always accept the superiority of truth to fiction. Herodotus often tells lengthy stories he admits are false, disproves plausible stories, or accepts preposterous ones without proof. Yet Herodotus does sometimes make distinctions between real and fictional characters and events. He also on occasion mentions plausible—and by modern standards highly reasonable—criteria, which he says he uses to select his material. But Herodotus' statements about his discrimination between truth and falsehood are inconsistent and do not reflect his actual practice. As a result, readers have adopted widely divergent opinions about the writer's veracity and reliability. Some praise his judiciousness and impartiality and others, whose wholly different interpretation reveals the crux of the problem, call him a liar and a gullible fool.[1]

For the archaic Greeks, poems or *muthoi*—what we would call fictions—did not possess the same kind of reality as everyday experience, but *muthoi* were not therefore wholly false. Yet until Plato and perhaps not even then, the Greeks did not develop any consistent terminology to describe and discriminate between factual and other kinds of truth.[2] Thucydides, for example, must labor with periphrases like ἡ ζήτησις τῆς ἀληθείας (1.20) or τὴν ἀκρίβειαν αὐτὴν τῶν λεχθέντων, "the very exactness of what was said" (1.22), to convey the idea of historical accuracy in his reporting of speeches.[3] Nor did the kind of truth that we consider closest to reality—whether we call it literal, factual, or historical—enjoy any automatic primacy. Rather, in rhetoric *eikos*, "likelihood," and in poetry a kind of artistic truth according to which fictions were assumed to be somehow wise, had by Herodotus' day achieved the greatest sophistication and prestige. Plato (*Phaedrus* 267A) says of the rhetoricians Gorgias and Tisias, contemporaries of Herodotus, who wrote both speeches and technical treatises about their art: "They saw that what is likely [τὰ εἰκότα] is more worthy of honor than what is true [τῶν ἀληθῶν]."[4] Though Hecataeus writes what he thinks is true, he apparently applies no other test than likelihood to his materials.

Earlier, Hesiod's muses proudly claim fiction, ψεύδεα πολλὰ . . . ἐτύμοισιν ὁμοῖα, "many falsehoods equivalent to truth," as their special gift, but they assign literal truth, which in this context means only correct, practical information, a secondary importance (*Theogony* 27–28).[5] The early Greeks valued the ability to tell stories, not to be confused with malicious lying, as a special and distinguished talent. Nestor's skill at ψεύδεα πολλὰ . . . ἐτύμοισιν ὁμοῖα, "falsehoods equivalent to truths," Theognis ranks with such other envied human *aretai* as the "wisdom of Rhadymanthus" and "the swiftness of the children of Boreas" (699–728).

Moreover, the Greeks took for granted a listener's ability to discern the truths embedded in fiction. Greek education consisted chiefly of memorizing famous poetry, and Aristophanes and even a hostile critic like Plato assume that the purpose of speaking and hearing poetry is to realize and act on truths illustrated by stories and myths.[6] In Book 19 of the *Odyssey*, the disguised Odysseus tells Penelope ψεύδεα πολλὰ . . . ἐτύμοισιν ὁμοῖα (19.203), a false tale about his capture by pirates and other made-up adventures. Odysseus' tale, intimately connected to and reminiscent of his real adventures,

serves both to comfort Penelope with the news her husband
may still be alive and to test her faithfulness as Odysseus watch-
es her reactions.[7] In comparison with this sophisticated story,
with its subtle purpose and underlying connections with reality,
Hecataeus' claim to tell "the truth as I see it," ὥς μοι δοκεῖ
ἀληθέα εἶναι (F.1), which he follows with a simplistic rationalization of myth, must have seemed pitifully naive to Herodotus and many other Greeks.[8] It is no wonder that Herodotus makes no assumption that verifiable facts possess an
intrinsic superiority to fictions as a means of seeking and telling
the truth about human life.

On the other hand, the subject that inspires Herodotus, the Persian wars, was a real event and close enough to
Herodotus' lifetime to have left living witnesses and concrete
evidence, although Marathon and Salamis were just far enough
in the past not to be part of Herodotus' own memory.[9] A
modern historian of the recent past would take the surviving
reliable evidence, however scanty, and construct the best and
most trustworthy account based only on that evidence. Heir to
the Greek storytelling tradition, however, Herodotus regards
the characters of men—and not just the most important men—
as a key to history just as the storyteller does for his tale. But
reliable information about the true character and personality of
such men as Themistocles and Xerxes was just the kind of
evidence that had scarcely survived down to Herodotus' day.

Because he sees traces of the fire on the Acropolis,
Herodotus can authenticate reports that the Persians sacked
Athens (5.77). Because in his day the Plataeans are still plowing
up Persian treasure and human bones from the battlefield, Herodotus can verify that a real battle took place there (9.83). Of
course in Herodotus' day no one could have maintained that
the sack of Athens or the battle of Plataea were fictional events.
Rather, the physical survivals impressed upon Herodotus the
contrast between recent, verifiable history and the unreliable
earlier period, too remote in antiquity to leave any visible
traces. Herodotus does use such evidence to distinguish real
from mythical events, but he is not willing to make such objective evidence the sole basis for what he writes, because this

evidence gives no insight into the psychology of individuals. To answer the questions Herodotus wants to ask about the personalities of the men who fought the Persian wars, he can only turn, in the absence of the wealth of personal memorabilia available to the historian today, to anecdotes: brief stories that illuminate the psychology of individuals. Herodotus himself recognizes the historical limitations of these anecdotes; but he believes that they can reveal important truths about real men and their motives, even if the stories themselves are not literally true.

      Herodotus uses caution in accepting either kind of evidence, facts or anecdotes. Facts he may not deny, but their significance, he realizes, may sometimes be slight. Although he will adopt a rationalist approach where it suits his purposes, he will not on every occasion use rationalism to reduce an anecdote to bare facts. As Hecataeus' example demonstrated, the search for the facts may turn up conclusions too trivial to warrant the effort. Nevertheless, parallel to his anecdotal narrative, Herodotus constantly refers to factual evidence such as surviving artifacts or monuments in order to keep the actuality of the Persian wars before his reader. He never loses sight of the difference between myth and history. He never forgets that he is describing a real event. Furthermore, he is not interested in just a good story—any more than Odysseus just makes up an entertaining yarn for Penelope. Herodotus chooses to tell the stories that are richest in the themes and motifs he finds most revealing about human life. These are *his* "falsehoods equivalent to truths," ψεύδεα ἐτύμοισιν ὁμοῖα. In his anecdotes, however, he will at times appear to the reader to have knowledge he cannot possibly possess and must even contradict what physical evidence proves real and true. A lesser writer might have chosen to ignore or gloss over such contradictions between truth and fiction. Herodotus wittily calls attention to them.

      In fact, I believe contradictions between truth and fiction throughout the *Histories* constitute a key unifying pattern. Herodotus constantly questions the validity of both facts and anecdotes as evidence for history. For him, on different occasions, both kinds of evidence or only one can contribute to an understanding of events. In constantly juxtaposing, comparing, and criticizing both categories of evidence Herodotus characteristically uses irony to point out those instances where the truth is trivial, where fiction is silly, or where neither gives insight. As we shall see, his irony is most intense at those moments in his *Histories* when there is a maximum divergence between the artistic truth of the anecdotal tradition and the literal truth revealed by physical evidence or the test of common sense.

Herodotus thus attempts—in a style unique to him—to bridge the gap between the historian's task, which according to Aristotle is to present what really happened, and the task of the poet, which Aristotle says is to present the possibilities of what might have happened (*Poetics* 1451b). Yet as we shall see in the passages examined in this chapter, Herodotus implicitly admits, often in an ironic and playful fashion, the impossibility of bridging this gap between truth and fiction. At the same time, he rejects the simple-mindedness of ignoring the facts altogether or of valuing the facts alone and rejecting all fictions. His self-conscious irony about the relation between fact and fiction puts Herodotus in a singular middle ground between the historical novelist, who tries to obscure from his reader the point at which the evidence stops and his invention begins, and the conventional historian, who professes to eschew invention altogether.

Three related anecdotes in the *Histories* show how Herodotus contrasts two versions of events, one dramatic and interesting but untrue, and the other trivial and uninteresting but true. Like the Persian *aitia* and Gyges stories, anecdotes of this type serve in the *Histories* in place of the direct, programmatic statements about method and theory that we find in Thucydides and other historians.

These three anecdotes belong to a larger group of stories that illustrate the motif of a king crossing water.[10] The story of Xerxes bridging the Hellespont supplies, of course, the major example of the motif, and to this passage all others look forward or back. According to the normal pattern of this group, a king crosses a river or sea boundary in unusual circumstances or with the help of a wise adviser or some ingenious mechanical device. Inevitably there is a mood of foreboding, for the king violates a national boundary or *nomos* by his crossing. Three stories that illustrate this motif, however, form a special category because they share an extra feature. In each case Herodotus gives two versions of how the king crosses the boundary: a colorful and minute version that he calls false, and a dull and matter-of-fact version that he calls true. In these three stories Herodotus tells the false version in surprising detail given his statement or his proof that the story is wrong.

When Herodotus begins the story of how Croesus crosses the Halys to attack Cyrus (1.75), he states his own estimate of what actually happened: "*I* say he crossed on the bridges that were there at the time": ὡς μὲν ἐγὼ λέγω κατὰ τὰς ἐούσας γεφύρας, but then he goes on to tell "the story common among the Greeks," ὡς δὲ ὁ πολλὸς λόγος Ἑλλήνων, that Thales the Milesian engineered the crossing. Next Herodotus gives an account of how the army *did not* cross the Halys with the help of Thales. This description occupies about fifteen lines in our modern texts, but the account of how the army *did* cross—over the bridges—amounts to only four words: κατὰ τὰς ἐούσας γεφύρας. Herodotus describes Thales' ingenuity with great attention to specific details. Croesus reaches the river, and since there are no bridges, "falls into perplexity." But Thales, who "happens to be present," gives assistance: "It is said that, beginning above the army, he dug a deep trench, running it in a half-moon course so that it would pass behind the encamped army and in this way turn the river out of its original stream down the trench and then, having passed the army, come out again into its original channel so that as soon as the river was split it became fordable on either side" (1.75.5–6). This long, sinuous sentence, which mimics the course of the water channel it describes, is remarkable for describing in such detailed intricacy a channel that never existed. Equally remarkable, given his explicit rejection of the story, is the writer's subsequent quibbling with those who claim that Thales' channel completely drained the Halys, "for how," complains Herodotus, "could they have crossed back over again?" (1.75.6).

The second anecdote of this group describes the crossing not of a river or strait but of a desert, where, paradoxically, lack of water is the obstacle that must be surmounted. To attack the Egyptians, Cambyses must cross the Arabian desert, which presents the same kind of natural boundary as those that Croesus, Xerxes, and the other kings must conquer in their quests for expansion beyond their proper boundaries (3.9). The details invite us to compare this desert with other, water boundaries. Here again, it is a question of whether Cambyses crosses this boundary by the usual means, recalling "the bridges that were there at the time" in the story of Thales above, or whether he crossed by extraordinary and ingenious means. Herodotus first tells the truth: Cambyses supplies his army with water and thus effects the crossing by sending ahead caravans of camels and other pack animals laden with skins of water to establish supply depots (3.9.1). This first account is utterly convincing and plausible. But now Herodotus makes a surprising statement: "This is the more credible [ὁ πιθανώτερος] of the stories told, but the less credible [τὸν ἧσσον πιθανόν], since people also tell it [ἐπεί γε δὲ λέγεται], must [δεῖ] be narrated" (3.9.2). This less credible version is once again a story of ingenuity told in great detail: Cambyses has constructed "a conduit of sewn untanned cowhide and other skins" in order to convey water from the river Corys to the desert. He also has large reservoirs (δεξαμενάς) built to collect and store the water. Herodotus specifies the amazing distance, a twelve-days journey, from the river to the desert and notes that actually there were three different conduits to three different reservoirs: δι' ὀχετῶν τρι-ῶν ἐς τριξὰ χωρία (3.9.2–4).[11]

The third anecdote of this group, the "captain's reward," tells of Xerxes' flight from Greece after the defeat at Salamis. Herodotus, after finishing his account of the retreat of Xerxes by land to Asia, tells us "there is another story told," ἔστι δὲ καὶ ἄλλος ὅδε λόγος λεγόμενος (8.118). Xerxes did not cross back over the river Strymon by the bridges earlier constructed for him on his march from Asia, and which elsewhere Herodotus describes in detail (7.24–25, 113), but he sailed from the western shore of the Strymon in a Phoenician ship with a large retinue of Persian nobles.

A gale strikes the ship and a terrified Xerxes asks the captain if there is hope. "There is none," the captain replies, "unless we can somehow get rid of these numerous passengers." Xerxes appeals to his royal entourage: "Men of Persia, let every one of you who truly cares for his king now show it, for it appears that my safety is in your hands" (118.3). The Persians immediately prostrate themselves and jump overboard to their deaths, thus allowing the ship to reach shore safely. Xerxes' actions at this point provide the story with its startling dénouement: "Because he had saved the king's life, Xerxes gave the captain a golden crown, but because the man had caused the death of many Persians, he cut off his head" (118.4).

Herodotus now proceeds at length and in detail to demolish the historicity of the story, calling it "completely unbelievable in my opinion" because "not one man in ten thousand" would believe that Xerxes sacrificed valued Persians when he could have had the lowly and numerically inferior Phoenician sailors pitched overboard instead. Herodotus now reasserts ("just as I said before") the truth of the story of Xerxes' crossing of the Strymon by bridges (119). He even adduces physical evidence for Xerxes' route. He cites a gold axe and tiara the Persian king gave to the residents of Abdera, a town he would not have visited if the story of crossing the Strymon by ship were true. Only in one small detail does Herodotus criticize the "true" version of Xerxes traveling by land and stopping at Abdera: he doubts the Abderites' claim that Xerxes "first loosed his girdle there [in Abdera]" (120).

Once again we have both a plausible and an unusual version of the king's journey. Here, too, Herodotus compares the literal truth, as he sees it, with a reported story. This story he tells in colorful detail, and the vivid dialogue of the anecdote parallels the role of the elaborate physical descriptions in the Thales and Cambyses passages. In particular, the ingenuity of the captain, who plays the role of a wise adviser, recalls the ingenuity of Thales and Cambyses in crossing the Halys and the Arabian desert.[12] Here, too, Herodotus doubts the veracity of the more colorful version and musters much contrary evidence to prove the unreliability of the account: his own doubt, the unlikelihood of the event, his own doubt again in the form of an emphatic denial, and the physical evidence against it. In all three cases, moreover, what Herodotus says actually did happen is not just less interesting but dull and trivial. Other than asserting that these events in fact happened, Herodotus never tries to attach any importance to the fact that Croesus crossed the bridges, that Cambyses arranged water caravans, or that Xerxes went by land and not by sea.

The most important similarity linking these stories, however, is that Herodotus in all three professes to doubt a story that contains ideas and themes he elsewhere accepts. First of all, the three versions Herodotus rejects all follow the pattern of the motif "king crosses water," and they serve to remind us of Cyrus crossing the Araxes to attack the Massagetae (1.208), Darius crossing the Ister to attack the Scyths (4.89), and especially Xerxes crossing the Hellespont to attack the Greeks (7.56). Croesus—with Thales' help—and Cambyses act contrary to nature and even improperly in diverting these bodies of water from their customary channels.[13] Their acts unmistakably prefigure Xerxes' arrogant taming of the Hellespont. Even Herodotus' interest in the specific materials used in Cambyses' water conduits suggests a comparison with the writer's detailed description of the complex construction of the cables anchoring Xerxes' pontoon bridge (7.36). In addition, the refutation of the anecdote of the "captain's reward" touches on the Asian terminus of this bridge—Abydos. Furthermore, the storm that, according to the story, threatens Xerxes as he crosses the Strymon and the beheading of the sea captain recall similar events earlier in the crossing of the Hellespont: a gale swept away Xerxes' first bridge, and to punish the architects responsible, Xerxes had them beheaded (7.35).

The "captain's reward" in particular seems thematically suited to Herodotus' narrative because this rejected version contains a number of ideas about Xerxes, the Persians, and life in general that Herodotus elsewhere indicates are true and significant. First, the story illustrates extreme opposites—kindness and cruelty, laughter and tears, cleverness and folly—of a type that Herodotus relishes in general and associates especially with Xerxes.[14] Second, the story reveals, as do others in the *Histories,* the cowardice of Xerxes. Herodotus has earlier shown us how eagerly after his defeat at Salamis Xerxes seizes upon the advice of Mardonius and Artemisia to retreat quickly to Asia and leave the fighting to them. "Even if every man and woman had urged him to remain," remarks Herodotus, "he would not have done so: so great was his fear" (8.103). Such a man might well panic in a storm at sea or retreat in terror all the way to Abdera without stopping. Nevertheless, Herodotus skeptically questions this very detail. The Persians in the sea captain story, true to their character elsewhere, slavishly obey capricious orders, and the captain's fate demonstrates another recurrent motif in Herodotus: the suddenness with which calamity may follow good fortune.[15] Most of all, this story reveals Xerxes' stupidity, for he foolishly sacrifices Persians instead of Phoenicians and kills a man whose advice has saved his life and who might be useful to him in the future. Xerxes' whole life, as Herodotus describes it, shows one such miscalculation after another, particularly in his estimate of his resources. This story also unforgettably illustrates, by means of the sea captain's crowned but decapitated head, Xerxes' fickleness, a mixture of generosity and cruelty.

The "captain's reward," an incident in Xerxes' flight from Greece, also perfectly fits the structure of this part of the *Histories* by forming the counterpoint to another story of generosity and cruelty during Xerxes' journey *to* Greece. This story, of Pythius the Lydian, precedes and thematically mirrors the "captain's reward." Pythius, like the captain, offers Xerxes aid, money to defray the costs of the expedition (7.27). Pythius, in fact, offers Xerxes his entire store of gold and silver, whose exact amount he proudly recites (7.28). Xerxes reacts to this offer with a combination of kindness and savagery that foreshadows his behavior to the sea captain. Xerxes takes Pythius' offer literally, although we may suppose that it is only an oriental host's conventional hospitality, which expects a refusal. In this case Pythius' extreme politeness may be a canny plan to forestall confiscation. If so, the plan works, for Xerxes expresses delight with the offer but graciously refuses. Instead, the king, in a matching gesture of generosity, gives Pythius enough money to bring his fortune to the next highest round figure (7.29). When Pythius now asks, however, to have his son stay behind and not march with the king's army to Greece, Xerxes flies into a fury and has the boy executed (7.38–39).

Another link subtly connects the story of Pythius with the "captain's reward," for the anecdote about Pythius, split into two sections, virtually coincides with Herodotus' description of the crossing of the Hellespont. By associating the Pythius story with the true account of Xerxes crossing the Hellespont, he associates it with the false account of Xerxes crossing the Strymon as well. In fact, if we look at the sequence of events early in Book Seven, immediately before and after the Hellespont passage, we find a series of related themes that look both forward and back in the *Histories*. They also reveal that Herodotus has carefully planned his narrative to illustrate the interrelated motifs of "crossing the river" and "kindness and cruelty." It is here (7.25) that he first describes the linen and flax bridges that Xerxes, before leaving Sardis, orders built across the Strymon for later use. The details look back to Cambyses' ingenious hose across the Libyan desert and forward to the much more elaborate Hellespont bridge and even further forward to the story of the "captain's reward," for these are the bridges that Xerxes will cross when he does *not* return by sea. Then there follows the first part of the story of Pythius, Xerxes' gift (7.27–29). At this point, however, the story breaks off, to be continued a short while later. Now Herodotus describes Xerxes' crossing of the Hellespont (7.30–37) and then resumes the story of Pythius with the Lydian's request and his son's death (7.38–39). A crucial event in the crossing of the Hellespont is an eerie eclipse that unnerves Xerxes and leads him to consult the Magi (7.37). This occurrence provides a thematic link with the Pythius story, for though the Magi interpret the omen to mean doom for Greece, a doubt arises in Xerxes' mind, which finds expression in his wrathful response to Pythius' request to spare his son the risk of fighting in Xerxes' war.

Here, then, are three anecdotes, of Croesus, Cambyses, and Xerxes, in which Herodotus has pitted a story of great artistic significance and truth for the *Histories* against strong arguments that it is false. The more artistically significant the story, the more elaborate Herodotus' refutation. Herodotus, in fact, expends almost as many words disproving the story of the "captain's reward" (162) as he does telling it (168). He also balances truth and falsehood in other ways in these stories, for the details of the significant, colorful tales are bizarre enough to make the reader incredulous, while his refutations often make use of a wayward and capricious logic that compromises the conclusiveness of his argument. Thales' and Cambyses' stratagems appear to be fantastic marvels rather than bold engineering projects actually capable of being achieved. In comparison with the subtle moral questions suggested by the story of Pythius (did Pythius really expect Xerxes to take his money? was Xerxes' subsequent anger completely unjustified?), Herodotus turns the story of the "captain's reward" into a joke. He represents, for example, Xerxes' decision both to put a crown on the head of the captain and to have that head cut off as a single act of judgment. The quality of the arguments used to refute these stories strikes us as hollow. It seems strange that Herodotus should seriously quibble whether Thales' ditch totally drained the Halys from its original channel if the whole story is untrue in any case. If the Halys could be turned completely into a ditch to allow Croesus to reach Persia, it could presumably be turned back again to allow him to cross on his return. Similarly, Herodotus leaves many holes in the logic of his refutation of the "captain's revenge." Commentators have, in fact, complained that the very point on which Herodotus is so sure—that Xerxes would have sacrificed Phoenicians and not Persians—is open to doubt, for the Persian courtiers would hardly have performed adequately as sailors in the storm.[16] Furthermore, Herodotus withholds criticism from the story's most unbelievable feature, the combination of award and execution. Should Herodotus not ask of what use a golden crown will be to a man with no head?

Now we can look with renewed interest and a better understanding at other passages in the *Histories* where, as in the three anecdotes just analyzed, Herodotus implicitly or explicitly comments on the truth or falsehood of his narrative. Of particular interest among such comments are passages where Herodotus professes that he is merely handing on to his reader τὰ λεγόμενα, "what people say," and implies or says that this narrative is not necessarily true. In virtually all these passages, in my opinion, Herodotus comments on truth and falsehood to show the reader, often by posing the same antithesis between dull fact and colorful falsehood analyzed above, that the truth is not simple but complex. Such passages, therefore, speak to the writer's sophisticated and ironic insouciance and not to his scientific objectivity ("I will present *all* the evidence") or to his naiveté ("I cannot resist telling you this even though it is not true").

The two statements below, frequently quoted by scholars, set forth Herodotus' principles about his criteria or lack of criteria for selecting his material:

> Anyone who believes things like this is welcome to do so, but the principle underlying my whole work is that I write what I hear each of my informants tell me [τὰ λεγόμενα]. (2.123)

> I am bound to report what my informants tell me [τὰ λεγόμενα] but I am definitely not bound to believe it all and this applies to my whole work. (7.152)

In fact, the phrase τὰ λεγόμενα—"what my informants tell me"—occurs often enough in the *Histories* to constitute a noticeable refrain: "I can only report *what my informants tell me*" (2.130). "I cannot say anything except *what my informants tell me*" (6.137).

Another group of passages that should be considered at the same time as these statements appears to convey Herodotus' feeling that he *must* write down not just what he thinks is the likely and correct version of events but also whatever incorrect and unlikely stories he hears. At times he even says explicitly that he feels obligated to give all possible versions. For instance, Herodotus says he *must* (δεῖ) tell the less believable account of how Cambyses crossed the desert (3.9). In his account of how the Spartans gave up their siege of Samos simply from lack of success (3.56.1), Herodotus adds another version even though he calls it "rather ridiculous" (ματαιότερος) in which Polycrates bribes the Spartans with counterfeit money to depart (3.56.2). His desire to include evidence he judges "ridiculous" seems to show a feeling of obligation to report the total evidence. Similarly, Herodotus appears to believe that versions of events reported only by a minority of sources have as much right to be heard as those that are on every man's lips. For example, Herodotus gives two reasons why Oroetes wants to depose Polycrates: "That is the reason most people give . . . but a few people say . . . and you may believe whichever of these versions you like" (3.120–122).

Many readers of Herodotus have believed that such passages amount to a pledge by the author to give us, to the best of his ability, *all* the evidence: every version of every story and every fact he ever heard. Exactly this presumption leads Rawlinson to interpolate the word "all" into one of the passages quoted above so that it reads: "My duty is to report *all* that is said" (7.152).[17] We cannot, I believe, accept such statements uncritically.

Herodotus' actual practice plainly contradicts the assumption that his goal is to preserve all the evidence and give all possible versions of an event. Yet the idea that Herodotus is a thorough and methodical collector of evidence, who wishes to present and preserve all alternatives for the reader, is entrenched enough to require some explanation of its origins in order to dislodge it. First, critics have based their theories and assumptions on only a very few passages. In one often-cited article on Herodotus' assessment of variant versions, such a conclusion as "Herodotus always tried to make an intelligent, thoughtful choice based on his researches" is drawn from a study of four passages in the *Histories* and a citation of only twelve more.[18] There are in the *Histories* many more explicit statements about truth and falsehood than these, and even more implied judgments. To identify all of them is admittedly subjective, but by my own reckoning at least seventy-five passages need to be considered before drawing any conclusions about Herodotus' attitude to truth and falsehood. Second, scholars have too often accepted without question Herodotus' own statements about his methods of sifting evidence and not tested those statements by examining his actual treatment of evidence in the *Histories*. Third, we have come almost full circle from the nineteenth-century view of Herodotus as "father of lies" (partly because of some twentieth-century discoveries that proved Herodotus was an accurate observer where he had been presumed to be fabricating). Now we are predisposed against all likelihood to assume that Herodotus must be interested in truth in exactly the same way as a modern historian.[19] Fourth, many studies that attribute to Herodotus a rigorous and rational (though I would say simple-minded) attitude to the weighing of evidence have focused all but exclusively on Book Two, although the rest of the *Histories* offers much important evidence on historical method.[20] Such studies have not fully taken into account that Herodotus' practice in Book Two is, for special reasons, not altogether typical. Herodotus takes a particular, malicious pleasure in Book Two in proving the Egyptians absolutely right and the Greeks absolutely wrong on a number of topics, especially about the story of Helen of Troy. Therefore, no theory about truth and falsehood in Herodotus should be based substantially on the Helen passage, for example, or on any other passage in Book Two.[21]

In addition, many studies of Herodotus make questionable assumptions about his supposedly omnivorous appetite for the marvelous. It would be impossible for Herodotus or any writer, however Proustian his style and memory, to tell us all he heard, even in a book much longer than the *Histories*. Some considerable selection, even if unconscious, is inevitable. Herodotus, in fact, specifically tells us in a number of passages that he has selected his material from a larger body of evidence. He does not tell us, for example, "the story of Abaris" (4.36), whatever that may have been. He tells us that he learned the names of all the 300 Spartans who died at Thermopylae (7.224), but he does not give these names. Other examples of explicit omissions are the Samian who expropriated the wealth of Sataspes' eunuch (4.43), the Greeks who claimed as their own the Egyptian doctrine of metempsychosis (2.123), and the Delphian responsible for forging an inscription (1.51).[22] Herodotus recognizes selection from among variants as an artistic prerogative when he mentions that Homer knew another version of the events of the Trojan war but rejected it as not εὐπρεπής, "appropriate," to his poem (2.116). He himself says at one point, in passing, that he will go no further on a certain topic since he is not compelled to do so by the ἀναγκαίη, "necessity," of his work (7.96). One of my aims here, therefore, is to identify the nature of this ἀναγκαίη or principle of selection by comparing Herodotus' explicit statements with his actual practice.

The most memorable and clearest case of Herodotus' practice of selection and omission on what we might call artistic grounds occurs in the story of Cyrus. Here the writer says that he knows "three other versions in addition," καὶ τριφασίας ἄλλας λόγων ὁδούς. But, Herodotus tells us, he will give us "the true story," τὸν ἐόντα . . . λόγον (1.95). At the end of the story, after Cyrus' death and the gruesome treatment of his corpse, Herodotus says—though he does not tell us what the other versions were—that the account he has just given is "the most credible of many stories told," πολλῶν λόγων λεγομέν-ων . . . πιθανώτατος (1.214.5).

If, then, Herodotus often violates his promise to include the untrue along with the true, how do we account for his claim to give "what my informants tell me," and how can we explain why he tells some untrue versions and not others? My answer is, first, that a statement such as "This is only what they told me—don't ask me to believe it" is not intended to be taken literally or seriously because it is only a traditional raconteur's trick of punctuating a story with a disclaimer, usually at the beginning or end but sometimes in the middle of the tale. By this disclaimer the raconteur either alerts his audience to a particularly unusual—and therefore interesting—story, or releases harmlessly some of the tension of disbelief that builds up in an audience; if the disclaimer falls in the middle of an anecdote, he draws attention to some particularly bizarre detail.[23] Second, Herodotus elevates this stock phrase ("Don't ask me to believe all this") from a storyteller's attention-getting trick into an ironic comment on the problematic relation between truth and fiction. To demonstrate the first of these points we need only look at the contexts of the two passages quoted above in which Herodotus claims to tell only τὰ λεγόμενα. Although in these passages he specifically states that the principle λέγειν τὰ λεγόμενα underlies his whole work, in each case an unusual or outrageous story just narrated provides the actual occasion for the disclaimer.

The first of the two passages, in Book Two, caps a series of tall tales associated with the Egyptian pharaoh, Rhampsinitus, the famous tale of the robber of the king's treasury along with, as a coda, the report that Rhampsinitus was even said to have descended into Hades and played dice with Ceres (2.122). The second of the statements comments on the politically delicate question of the neutrality of Argos in the Hellenic resistance against Persia. The Argives, says Herodotus, claim they remained neutral only because of an oracle from Delphi (7.148). Herodotus, however, gives enough other information, including conversations overheard many years afterward at Susa, to indicate that he believes the Argives' neutrality was self-serving (7.151). Still, he says "I will not make any further comment on this other than what the Argives say [οὐδέ τινα γνώμην περὶ αὐτῶν ἀποφαίνομαι ἄλλην γε ἢ τήν περ αὐτοὶ 'Αργεῖοι λέγουσι]. But this much I know, if all men gathered their own sins and piled them up together to trade with their neighbors, they would gladly carry their own back home again once they got a look at the faults of others. So what the Argives did was really not so shameful after all" (7.152). In other words, Herodotus' claim—which follows at this point in the text—that he is bound to report the *legomena* of the Argives is clearly as ironic and unscientific as what he implies about Rhampsinitus, for in neither case does he credit in the slightest the literal truth of these stories.

Herodotus' statements that the principle λέγειν τὰ λεγόμενα guides him as an author are clearly ironic since, as we have seen, some selection is unavoidable, and the writer explicitly alludes to information he has been told but will not tell us. It is, in fact, typical of Herodotus to apply a statement like "I can only write what my informants tell me" not to historical subjects such as accounts of battles and political maneuvering but to such trivial questions as whether the Carchedonian maidens really do extract gold from a lake bottom with feathers dipped in pitch (4.195).

What influences Herodotus to include some false versions and not others? Despite the commonly held view that he is unable to resist any really good story, Herodotus' false versions of events almost always contain clearly identifiable themes that are significant in the *Histories* as a whole. The historian's reason for telling a false version is therefore literary and artistic. The *legomena* of the Egyptians, for example, demonstrate the ingenuity of the resourceful thief and the heroic self-sacrifice of his accomplice, both common Herodotean themes. The *legomena* of the Argives show the human failing of self-interest, a failing that we encounter in the *Histories* in such diverse characters as Gyges and Miltiades.

This literary purpose explains Herodotus' principle of selection in the case of variant versions. There are, I believe, three basic patterns: first, if Herodotus finds a version of a story that contains themes and ideas he believes significant and if he believes this version is also historically accurate (ὁ ἐὼν λόγος), or at least uncontradicted by factual evidence, he suppresses all other versions. Only rarely, as in the Cyrus story, does he mention the existence of variants without telling them. Indeed, the death of Cyrus with its triumph of a "clever, vengeful queen" could hardly be more likely, as we have seen in the last chapter, to appeal to Herodotus and crowd out all other variants from his text. But seldom does Herodotus even cite the existence of variants for his one-version stories. In this category, as in the Pythius story, he tells only one version of a story without criticism or reservation, for he has found that in this one version artistic and historical truth coincide. An extremely large

number of stories in the *Histories* fit this first category since it is
an exception—though certainly a significant one—for Herodotus actually to tell two versions of a story. But we cannot specify
exactly the size of this category, for in some cases, even where
we know of variants—in the Gyges story, for example—Herodotus may have heard only one version, found it suitable to his
Histories, and did not need to make any choice.[24] The single-
version story in Herodotus is the most straightforward, and
where that story is the result of the author's choice, the process
of selection is not surprising or in need of explication.

More remarkable is the second category: two versions of a story exist, neither is contradicted by material evidence, but both contain themes that interest Herodotus. In this
case Herodotus tells both versions without discrimination or
disclaimer. The example, noted above, of the two versions of
Oroetes' motives for attacking Polycrates fits this pattern, for it
ends with Herodotus' invitation to his readers to believe whichever version they prefer (3.122). Both versions show Oroetes
acting for hotheaded personal reasons: real or imagined slights
to his vanity. Both versions, therefore, present just the kind of
personal, emotional reasons for political events that Herodotus
promises his readers in the story of Gyges. In some of these
cases the possibility exists that Herodotus considers one of the
uncriticized variants also, by chance as it were, the literal truth,
ὁ ἐὼν λόγος. But if this is so, Herodotus never comments.

In the third pattern that illustrates Herodotus' principle of selection, the true facts, usually confirmed by material
evidence, do not contain significant motifs, but Herodotus
knows of or invents untrue stories that do contain them. Here,
as we have seen in the stories of Thales, Cambyses, and the
"captain's reward," Herodotus will tell the true version, citing
the available corroboratory evidence; but he also adds a significant though untrue version and often tells this untrue version in
considerable detail. This third category is remarkable and is the
cause of both criticism and puzzlement among Herodotus'
readers. For this reason, I have addressed it first in this chapter
with an analysis of three striking examples. Because Herodotus
deliberately tells stories he knows to be false, he seems to some
readers to be committing a greater sin than when he calls stories

true that modern readers now know to be false. But we should rather applaud Herodotus for his conscientiousness in including inconsequential and trivial facts that he might have easily and forgivably suppressed to give greater prominence to interesting ideas or motifs. But more than conscientiousness, I believe, leads Herodotus to tell the true along with the false. His deliberate narration of fictions is a conscious stylistic device that allows him to present and wittily emphasize an important difficulty that he recognizes in the nature of his evidence. Herodotus tells a colorful fiction but also includes the dull truth in order to present a neat antithesis between myth and history and to remind the reader that anecdotes and facts often have disparate interest and value. This antithesis between truth and fiction thus constitutes both a major theme and a significant literary device in the *Histories*.

Polycrates' bribery of the Spartans with counterfeit money (3.56) provides one more example of a passage in which Herodotus allows τὰ εἰκότα to stand on equal footing with τὰ ἀληθέα just as he does in the three stories that began this chapter. The truth is, Herodotus says, the Spartans simply gave up their siege of Samos (3.56.1). Given this fact, the story that they were bribed is ματαιότερος, "rather ridiculous" (3.56.2). Yet is it really ridiculous? Herodotus must be speaking ironically here, since elsewhere he shows us that the Spartans are quite susceptible to bribery and sufficiently unworldly in money matters (5.51) to accept counterfeit coins. Herodotus suggests, rather, that if the Spartans had not given up their siege and Polycrates had tried bribery, he probably would have succeeded. Furthermore, if the Spartans had not yielded, Polycrates, given what Herodotus tells us elsewhere of the Samian tyrant's wealth and guile (3.39), would probably have turned to bribery. If we may supply Herodotus with a word, these are τὰ εἰκότα, "what was likely" about the situation, for, even if literally untrue, they complete a picture of Polycrates and the Spartans that Herodotus clearly believes is true in a more general sense.

The category of uncriticized variants and two subcategories shed light on this characteristic Herodotean antithesis between true and false. The first subcategory involves statements of uncertainty about the truth of a story either with the phrase οὐκ ἔχω ἀτρεκέως λέγειν, "I cannot speak precisely," or by the author's inclusion of minor alternative details within a story. This characteristic allies this group closely with uncriticized variants. In the second subcategory Herodotus briefly but decisively denies the truth of a detail within a story but does not question the story, a variation on his technique in stories such as the "captain's reward."

Often Herodotus tells a story in two or more variants without any comment about their relative truth or falsity. Is he reluctant or for some reason unable to make a judgment? Yet these variant versions rarely present clearly opposed points of view or important contradictions but actually confirm a single point of view he wishes to establish.

For example, Herodotus tells how Cambyses murders his wife by kicking her in the stomach when she is pregnant. He assaults her, says Herodotus, because she provoked Cambyses by reminding him that he killed his brother to get the throne. Herodotus gives two versions of how the woman angers her husband. In the first she comments that Cambyses' brother had no sibling to aid him in his hour of need, unlike the puppy in a dog-and-lion fight the couple happen to be watching (3.32.1–2). In the second the wife, as she peels a head of lettuce, gets Cambyses to admit that the head was "lovelier" when intact. Then she reminds Cambyses that the house of Cyrus was also better intact (3.32.3–4). Both versions, and that is their purpose, make a similar point about Cambyses' violent and impetuous character, for in both accounts Cambyses reacts by killing his wife in a fit of rage. This fact Herodotus does not question. The effect of his alternative stories about Cambyses is not to introduce a note of caution or uncertainty about what actually happened, but just the opposite. He emphasizes Cambyses' stupidity and cruelty even more intensely through two stories with a similar point.[25]

Also similar in purpose are two versions of how a clever groom makes Darius' stallion neigh at the proper moment to proclaim his rider king (3.87). In one version the groom arranges for the fateful sunrise meeting of the seven conspirators to take place at a spot where the previous day the stallion had been allowed to cover his favorite mare (3.85–86). In a second version the groom, at the crucial moment, puts his hand, with which he has just touched the mare's genitals, over the stallion's nose (3.87). Here both stories make the same point: the groom is crafty and clever. Both stories also provide an earthy counterpart to the supernatural roll of thunder that follows and confirms Darius as king and to which Herodotus provides no alternatives (3.86.2).

Herodotus gives three versions of the origins of the Scyths (4.5–11). The first two versions present a standard case of the doublet or specious variation: two virtually identical folktales in which the youngest of three brothers is chosen king. In the first, golden talismans fall from the sky to announce the choice of the youngest (4.5). In the second, the youngest brother, son of Herakles and a local queen (who is half-snake), proves his worth by drawing a bow his father left behind (4.8–10). Herodotus clearly allows both these versions to stand in order to confer upon the Scyths, who are among the noblest of his savages, the accumulated prestige of two different stories of divine and magical origins. Thus Herodotus can give the Scyths both a human progenitor favored by the gods and a lineage traced back to Herakles. The theme of the test of the bow also links the Scyths to the Ethiopians, noble savages too, whose physical prowess is symbolized by their ability to use bows other races cannot even draw and whom Herodotus admires (3.21).

For the third version of Scythian origins Herodotus indicates a preference, though he makes no explicit judgment on its truth or falsehood: τῷ μάλιστα λεγομένῳ αὐτὸς πρόσκειμαι, "To this tale I am particularly inclined" (4.11.1). Herodotus expresses interest in the third version, I believe, because this story contains a significant Herodotean motif: a "brave gesture."[26] In addition, since the story deals not with the origins of the Scyths but with how they came to take up residence in the place where they now live, the third version need not preclude the truth of one or the other of the first two versions. Herodotus explains that the Scythian territory was originally inhabited by Cimmerians. The Scythians attack, and the Cimmerians fall into a dispute, the nobles wanting to stand and fight, the common people to withdraw. Finally, unable to persuade the others, the nobles decide to commit suicide (their brave gesture) rather than retreat or force their opinions on the common people, to whom the nobles say they owe a debt for good service through the years. The nobles kill one another in a mock battle down to and including the last man (4.11), surely a difficult feat, but Herodotus never questions it. Clearly, however, because they are all to some extent true, though in different ways, Herodotus allows all three versions to stand without criticism.[27]

Some Herodotean variant versions do present a more genuinely contradictory view of events, but there is always an underlying similarity. By refusing to choose between the variants, Herodotus asserts the importance of the common point. There are, for example, two accounts of how the golden bowl that the Spartans sent to Croesus came to be in Samos (1.70). The Spartans claim the Samians robbed them of the bowl on the high seas once it became known that Sardis had fallen and Croesus was already Cyrus' captive (1.70.2). But the Samians counter that the Spartans, having reached Samos en route to Sardis and having learned of Croesus' capture, sold the bowl to certain Samians, who brought it to the Heraeum in Samos (1.70.3). The Spartans calculated that on their return to the Peloponnesus they could say they had been robbed and pocket the money. By not exercising critical choice between these two discreditable accounts, Herodotus manages to criticize both Samians and Spartans. Although obviously both Samians and Spartans cannot have been guilty of what each accuses the other of doing, both groups, and perhaps other Greeks as well, are, Herodotus implies, quite capable of such acts of greed.[28] The story of the bowl's provenance thus provides a neat counterpoint to the story of the fall of Croesus, for the anecdote juxtaposes the petty venality and quarreling of the Greeks with the Lydian king's suffering and ennoblement.

As in the story of Cambyses' wife, the focus of Herodotus' interest is not on the details of either variant but on some fact or facts that the presence of variants takes for granted: the Spartans *did* send Croesus a bowl, but Sardis fell before it could be delivered. Herodotus relishes the irony of this story of a Spartan gift to Croesus because the Spartans are offering aid to a barbarian aggressor violating a natural boundary, the Halys. Croesus thus anticipates the role Xerxes will later play when he crosses the Hellespont to attack Greece. The Spartans—ironically, in view of their later heroism against the barbarians—anticipate the role of those Greeks, particularly the Ionians, who collaborate with Xerxes. That this bowl should only get halfway to Sardis before Croesus' downfall illustrates the characteristic dilatoriness of the well-meaning but slow Spartans (7.206; 9.7) and underscores the suddenness of Croesus' unexpected fall from prosperity into adversity.

A final example, the anecdote of the "two anchors of Sophanes" (9.74), shows how, by the end of Herodotus' *Histories,* the antithetical pattern of the significant but false versus the insignificant but true story can by itself guide the reader to determine Herodotus' implicit opinion. Of Sophanes Herodotus tells us there are "double stories," διξοὺς λόγους λεγομένους. The first is that he went into battle with an iron anchor chained around his waist. In combat he would "drop anchor," ἄγκυραν . . . βαλλέσκετο, so that the enemy could not budge him from his position. Then, he would "up anchor," τὴν ἄγκυραν ἀναλαβόντα, and pursue the enemy when they retreated.[29] Herodotus passes immediately to the second version, commenting only—with what seems to the reader to be considerable understatement—that this other version, τῷ πρό-τερον λεχθέντι ἀμφισβατέων λέγεται (9.74.2), "differs from the above." In the second version Sophanes only has an anchor emblazoned on his shield. Both these versions, one an imaginative but impossible fiction, the other highly plausible, Herodotus allows to stand without comment. Only in one tiny detail, the intrusion in a ὡς clause of the oblique infinitive of reported speech (when Sophanes picks up his anchor to "pursue," διώκειν, the enemy [9.74.1]), does Herodotus give a substantive clue—perhaps an unconscious one—of which version he believes credible.[30] By now Herodotus does not need to comment specifically on the truth or fiction of the story, for if we compare it with the "captain's reward" and related anecdotes, the pattern is so well established that we, like Herodotus, can see the plausible (but disappointing) truth in the prosaic account and the meaningful (but implausible) fiction in the romantic version. Taken literally, the "two anchors of Sophanes" is an uncriticized variant, but actually Herodotus' implicit judgment turns it into a sharp antithesis between truth and falsehood akin to that of the "captain's reward."

But precisely what significance does Herodotus find in Sophanes' "real" anchor? This humorous anecdote, I believe, burlesques Greek heroism. It is easy to imagine that by the late fifth century many sophisticated Greeks had tired of self-congratulatory recitals of Greek bravery in the Persian wars. This skeptical sentiment we find even in the speeches of Thucydides. Sophanes does not seem admirably superhuman in his heroism but silly, as he attempts to run in pursuit of the enemy and, as he goes, picks up and carries with him an anchor so heavy that it earlier rendered him immovable.[31]

At times Herodotus gives only a single version of events but admits to uncertainty about the whole or about details with the phrase οὐκ ἔχω ἀτρεκέως λέγειν, "I cannot say precisely." Because the *Histories* obviously includes much hearsay and conjecture, it is hard to credit the relatively small number of cases where Herodotus admits that he is not "unerringly" (ἀτρεκέως) sure.[32] The cases also tend to focus on minor or trivial problems whose resolution would add little to the narrative. Herodotus writes that he is not quite sure, for example, if all or only some of the nomad Lydians cauterize the veins of their children's heads (4.187) or exactly what language the Caunians speak (1.172). The contrast between the austere statement of scientific objectivity—ἀτρεκέως is common in the Hippocratic corpus—and the minor and trivial subjects it governs in the *Histories* points to a note of playfulness.[33]

Such expressions of caution have a literary purpose similar to that of the uncriticized variants. Herodotus' hesitancy about one detail lends greater credibility to other details that go unquestioned. He admits, for example, that he does not know exactly the *amount* of money, οὐ γὰρ ἔχω τοῦτό γε εἰπεῖν ἀτρεκέως, that the Mytilenians agreed to accept as a bribe to betray the suppliant Paktyas, but he does not question that a bribe was proposed (1.160). As to which of the Ionians was brave and which cowardly in the battle of Lade, Herodotus says he does not know exactly what to record, οὐκ ἔχω ἀτρεκέως συγγράψαι, because, he continues, "they blame one another," ἀλλήλους γὰρ καταιτιῶνται (6.14). Thus Herodotus makes clear that though he is not sure which were brave, he is quite sure some were cowards.

Herodotus says he cannot choose between the reasons why Xerxes hurls a silver cup, a gold krater, and a Persian sword into the Hellespont after he successfully bridges the strait: οὐκ ἔχω ἀτρεκέως διακρῖναι (7.54). Are these offerings to the sun, Herodotus asks, or is Xerxes repenting for having the Hellespont flogged? The effect of Herodotus' stated uncertainty about *why* Xerxes acted as he did and his presentation of an alternative is to make the reader accept without question that Xerxes did throw offerings into the Hellespont, did have the Hellespont flogged, did have fetters thrown into it, and did instruct his men to say: "Oh bitter waters, your master punishes you in this way because you wronged him when you had suffered no wrong from him!" (7.35). In addition, Herodotus introduces both a note of sympathy for Xerxes by saying that the king might have repented for his earlier deed, and a note of criticism by implying that he surely ought to have repented.

Not all the passages in which Herodotus states his uncertainty about the veracity of his material include ἀτρεκέως. Another common practice to attain the same effect is to present, without comment, one or more alternatives for a detail in a story that is otherwise left unquestioned. Herodotus uses these alternative details as a sophisticated literary device to add subtlety of characterization or to make a moral comment. For example, he offers not just two but three possibilities to explain why Cyrus intended to immolate Croesus after the fall of Sardis: he was offering *akrothinia* to a god; or he wished to fulfill a vow; or, having learned that Croesus was god-fearing (θεοσεβέα), he wanted to see if some magical power (τις τῶν δαιμόνων) would save him from death (1.86.2). This range of possibilities, each of which adds nuance to the scene, shows, I believe, that Herodotus wants us to accept all three possibilities: that Cyrus had vowed to some god that if he were victorious he would sacrifice Croesus as part of his *akrothinia* (the first two alternatives), but then, seeing Croesus on the pyre and learning his reputation, the thought occurred to Cyrus to test the loyalty of Croesus' god. Herodotus thus recalls Croesus' own test of Apollo at Delphi and presents Cyrus' ambivalent moral qualities. Like Croesus, Cyrus is both piously generous in his offerings to the god and thoughtlessly impious in his casual skepticism.

A similar example of alternative motivations occurs after the sacking of the Acropolis. Xerxes orders the Athenian exiles who are members of his entourage to perform sacrifices among the ruins, "either because a dream had appeared to him and had told him to or because it became a 'weight on his mind' [ἐνθύμιον] that he had burned the sanctuary" (8.54). We might think that the alternatives amount to the same point, but by separating them Herodotus gives us two reasons for sympathizing with Xerxes at the very moment when his actions are likely to have stirred the reader's antipathy. First, Herodotus suggests that a sense of guilt may have prompted Xerxes' actions. Through his foolishness Xerxes usually acts wrongly, but he possesses enough insight occasionally to perceive that he has done wrong. Second, by introducing the possibility of a (god-sent?) dream, Herodotus reminds us of those earlier dreams that urged and finally compelled Xerxes to attack Greece in the first place. Xerxes, after all, even at the moment of Persian triumph and Greek defeat, is a prisoner of fate.

In brief asides or parentheses in which Herodotus mentions without elaborate refutation that details in a story are οὐ πιστά, "not believable," we find him in a playful mood. Through this device he adds the spicy, racy, or personal details both writer and reader enjoy without the former having to vouch for them or the latter having to believe them. Herodotus uses this storytelling device to give details that he refuses to accept as historically accurate. The ideas or themes that such details introduce, however, Herodotus does believe can offer insights into characters or motives. For example, the ten-year-old Cambyses pledges to his mother to punish Egypt ἐπεὰν ἐγὼ γένωμαι ἀνήρ, "when I grow up," for the slight offered her by Cyrus who prefers an Egyptian concubine to her. Herodotus introduces this story with the words: λέγεται δὲ καὶ ὅδε λόγος ἐμοὶ μὲν οὐ πιθανός, "and this story too is told, not convincing in my opinion" (3.3). But he tells this story at some length and includes the kind of specific human detail that makes the reader begin to believe in it: the boy was "about" ten years old, and the women of the harem were amazed at his boldness. The themes of revenge and an irrationally twisted character suit Herodotus' picture of Cambyses even though he rejects the historicity of this event from the ruler's childhood. But the transition between this rejected anecdote and the next paragraph reveals that Herodotus has in fact accepted—whether consciously or unconsciously—the artistic truth of this story. He begins the next paragraph: "And *another* event happened which resulted in this attack on Egypt" (3.4.1). This incident of Cambyses' childhood promise to his mother is basically no more unbelievable than any other in Herodotus' description of this mad king's colorful career. By saying that he does not believe this one detail, however, he singles it out for special attention.

Herodotus makes similar disclaimers about details in stories that are plainly fictional for a similar literary and artistic purpose: to highlight the artistic truth of a detail by showing its historical inaccuracy. For example, Herodotus doubts that Psammetichus cut out the tongues of the women who watched over the children on whom he carried out his experiment to discover what language humans who had been raised in isolation would speak (2.2). Herodotus also doubts (οὐ πιστά) that Rhampsinitus sent his daughter to serve in a brothel in order for her to locate the robber of his treasury by asking each of her customers what was the wickedest act he had ever committed (2.121ε). Each of these disclaimers adds the perfect touch of artistic truth to the story, an artistic truth to which Herodotus draws our special attention by pointing out that it was historically *un*true. We are quite ready to believe, along with Herodotus, that Cambyses could have been motivated by incidents in his childhood or that Psammetichus and Rhampsinitus could have been cruel and arbitrary. Psammetichus, after all, has snatched babies from their mothers at birth and raised them in cruel and artificial isolation. To cut out the nurses' tongues would be right in character for the pharaoh and, in a sense, a wise precaution to prevent the women from compromising the scientific purity of the experiment.[34] If Rhampsinitus sends his daughter to a brothel, he is only following what in Herodotus appears to be an old Egyptian royal custom, for Cheops had his daughter work as a prostitute to raise money for his pyramid, and she even built a sizable monument of her own with her tips (2.126).[35]

The "incredible" phenomena at the fringes of the known world occupy a special place among Herodotus' statements that he cannot believe certain events or facts. He finds one-eyed men (3.116), feathers falling from the sky (4.31), the sun on the right when you sail around Africa (4.42), and bees infesting the land beyond Istria (5.10) all to be οὐ πιστά. But it is not so much that these phenomena are unbelievable per se as that it is appropriate, Herodotus feels, that there should be "incredible" things at the ends of the earth, just as it is appropriate for Egyptian pharaohs to do incredible things such as cutting out womens' tongues and sending daughters to brothels. In all these cases Herodotus' irony lies in his calling "unbelievable" as historical fact details that are in fact extremely believable (πιστά) as fiction and no more fantastic than much that we find Herodotus not doubting at all.

We have found the father of history guilty of sometimes preferring fiction to truth. The only more damning charge to bring is to accuse him of not taking the distinction between myth and history seriously. Yet humor is an important key to Herodotus' attitude to his work as a historian. This humor is not a light veneer of jokes and sly remarks gilding the *Histories*. It is a profound irony about the contradictions surrounding truth and fiction. Truth and fiction should stand in opposition, a quintessential antithesis, and so Herodotus presents this contrast in many of the anecdotes analyzed in this chapter. Yet fiction paradoxically often offers a more important category of historical truth than facts. The style of the anecdotes focuses the reader's attention on this paradox. Herodotus' solution to the problem of the difference between myth and history is not only to admit it but to emphasize it with a characteristically wry wit. He smiles.

3

Nature and Culture:
The Noble Savage
and the Prosperous Aggressor

The story of the struggle between the Greeks and the Persians is also the story of the conflict between nature and culture. Xerxes' attack on Greece is but one of a long series of wars or other acts of aggression in which a man of culture, whom I call the "prosperous aggressor," attacks a man of nature, the "noble savage." In anecdotes throughout the *Histories* Herodotus espouses now the cause of the prosperous aggressor, now that of the noble savage. He illustrates, in other words, the truth of two contradictory ideas: man is happier and more noble in a state of nature; civilization raises man above his brutish natural state.

The subject of this chapter is also significant because of Herodotus' shifting view of who plays each part, for not all Persians are prosperous aggressors and not all Greeks are noble savages. In fact, when we first meet the Persians in Book One, *they* are the noble savages while the Spartans, who ultimately become noble savages whom Herodotus admires, are, at their introduction in Book One, prosperous aggressors with designs

against their *more* savage neighbors, the Arcadians. Croesus begins this story of shifting roles when he attacks the noble savage
Persians. Next, the Persians, now corrupted by wealth and
transformed into prosperous aggressors themselves, attack the
Massagetae. The pattern continues in Book Three with Cambyses' attack on the Ethiopians and in Book Four with Darius'
assault on the Scythians. At the end of the *Histories,* the Greeks,
impoverished but morally superior, play the part of the noble
savage, but the Greeks do not consistently or inevitably have
this role in the *Histories.*

My first purpose in this chapter will be to analyze the
characteristic traits of the prosperous aggressor and the noble
savage. For the former there is really only one significant trait
with which Herodotus is concerned: extraordinary wealth. Although readers of Herodotus usually claim that he condemns
the limitless riches of the barbarian kings, I will try to show that
he attempts to present a more positive side as well. For the
latter, the noble savage, however, Herodotus gives a detailed
catalogue of their style of dress, their eating habits, their moral
code, and the social organization of their families and state. This
chapter, following Herodotus' own focus, will concentrate primarily on the noble savage, although, as will be apparent, the
picture of the noble savage often contributes to our understanding of the prosperous aggressor to whom he is diametrically opposed.

Second, I will show how the potential for exchange of
these roles between Greek and barbarian, an idea that Herodotus continually keeps before the reader through repeated anecdotes, leads inevitably to a pessimistic conclusion to Herodotus'
history: at the moment of their triumph as noble savages, the
Greeks are already on the brink of their transformation into
prosperous aggressors.

In the opening sentence of the *Histories* Herodotus
accepts the Greek view that divides mankind into Hellenes and
barbarians, τὰ μὲν Ἕλλησι, τὰ δὲ βαρβάροισι ("Greeks on the
one hand, barbarians on the other"), but readers of the *Histories*
have not always agreed as to where the writer's sympathies lie in
this contrast between "us" and "them." During the fifth century

the word βάϱβαϱος, originally merely an onomatopoetic term for non-Greek speakers, acquired a more abstract connotation of ethnic differences and, increasingly, a pejorative sense similar to the English word "barbarian."[1] Herodotus uses βάϱβαϱος in these two latter senses in addition to the first and thus appears to accept and perpetuate—at least in some passages in the *Histories*—his contemporaries' cultural chauvinism.[2]

In antiquity, however, many readers of Herodotus took a wholly opposite view of the writer's purpose. Such readers, focusing on passages where he appears to praise the Persians, saw Herodotus as a φιλοβάϱβαϱος, "barbarian-lover." Plutarch's essay, "On the Malice of Herodotus," and the titles of similar works that have not survived (for example, "On the Lies of Herodotus") show that early readers of the *Histories* reacted hostilely to Herodotus' remarks about Greek city states and for reasons of patriotism and loyalty tried to refute these insults.[3] In the attempt to reconcile these two contradictory views of Herodotus, a patriot and yet obviously also a "barbarian-lover," a number of different explanations have arisen. Some scholars view these contradictions as the result of Herodotus' careful scholarship and historical impartiality in reporting both favorable and unfavorable information about both Greeks and their adversaries. Others, in diametric opposition, criticize his naiveté and inability to sift, judge, and select the most plausible interpretation from conflicting evidence. Still others, who see contradictions as proof of the incompleteness or composite nature of Herodotus' work, argue that discrepancies reveal him in the process of developing from an impartial geographer and ethnographer to a highly partial national historian.[4]

But if, to suggest another approach, we see that Herodotus has throughout the *Histories* constructed an artistic contrast between prosperous aggressors and noble savages, to which the various wars between Hellenes and barbarians are subsidiary, some of the inconsistencies are resolved. In addition, we gain a new insight into the structure and intent of the work. Herodotus measures barbarians and Greeks not against one another but against the standard of the archetypal noble savage and prosperous aggressor. Although the Greeks win a

clear military victory over the barbarians, there is no comparable straightforward resolution to the conflict between the prosperous aggressor and the noble savage at the end of the *Histories*. Herodotus' intent, therefore, seems to have been to leave
his readers with an uncomfortable sense of tension and transition at the end of his book rather than with the satisfaction of
battles clearly and irrevocably won or lost.

In the *Histories* material wealth and luxury imply sophistication, refinement, culture, imperial power, vast size, and
technological and organizational superiority. As the key dis-
tinguishing traits, wealth and poverty separate not only Herodotus' prosperous aggressors from his noble savages and Greeks
from barbarians, but also different groups of Greeks and barbarians from one another. Riches and prosperity, not ethnic identity, stamp a civilized way of life. Yet Herodotus' contemporaries
did not discriminate clearly between wealthy, civilized for-
eigners and people lacking in material goods and advanced
culture. The Greeks did not distinguish, for example, between a
Babylonian astronomer and an African pygmy, both of whom
were βάρβαροι, just as they used the same word, Ἕλλην, to
describe the Athenian aristocrat and an Arcadian shepherd.[5] But
Herodotus focuses on (a) types of behavior—bravery or cowardice, (b) personal attributes—ignorance or sophistication, or (c)
general categories—wealth or poverty, to show that he rejects or
finds insignificant the traditional world view of Greeks versus
barbarians. Prosperous aggressors, both Greeks and barbarians,
are wealthy but indolent, and cowardly but sophisticated, whereas noble savages, both Greeks and barbarians, are poor but
tough, ignorant but brave.[6] Although none of these characteristic qualities is more crucial than wealth for our understanding of Herodotus and his point of view about barbarians and
Greeks, Herodotus feels ambivalent about wealth, for riches
symbolize both an enviable prosperity and a contemptible
luxury.

Herodotus does not, as he is often mistakenly assumed to do, condemn wealth absolutely. A number of important passages show that he admires the splendor that money can
buy. In Book One, for example, we find lists of the gold and

silver that Gyges and Croesus dedicated at Delphi (1.14, 50–51). Though these many precious objects testify for Herodotus to the vanity of their dedicators' wishes, the writer also finds them in themselves "most worthy of fame," μάλιστα μνήμην ἄξιον ἔχειν (1.14). His detailed descriptions, moreover, usually reveal a keener interest in the monetary value of objects than in any beauty or artistic worth.[7]

Since one of the main features of Herodotus' antithesis between Persians and Greeks is that the former are rich and the latter are poor, he gives special prominence to Delphi, an ideal place for him to see and reflect on the riches of the eastern empires and the comparative poverty of Hellas. Solid gold and silver offerings from Lydia pointed up the rugged simplicity, for example, of the statues of Cleobis and Biton. Herodotus has certainly seen those statues, for he tells the story of their dedication (1.31.5), a tale that he likely heard at the sanctuary. But he gives us no details about these statues since, carved of humble Argive stone, they are not evidently ἀξιοθέατα, "worth looking at" (cf., e.g., 1.14). For gold and silver objects at Delphi, however, Herodotus not only routinely mentions size and weight but also specifies their location in the sanctuary and even notes some changes in location.

Herodotus' admiration for riches applies to Greeks as well as barbarians. He clearly admires Polycrates for his building projects (3.60) as well as his patronage of literature (3.122): "He was foully murdered [διεφθάρη κακῶς] in a way unworthy of him and his high resolve [φρονημάτων]. Except for the Syracusan tyrants not one of the Greek tyrants is worthy to be compared to Polycrates for magnificence [μεγαλοπρεπείην]" (3.125).[8] Although controversy surrounds his attitude to the Alcmaeonids, Herodotus does not condemn the eponymous Alcmaeon for filling his pockets with Persian gold (6.125). Herodotus seems to find in this particular story one more illustration of the immense gap in wealth that separates East from West, for Alcmaeon can establish his family's fortunes with a sum from the Persian treasury, whose loss the king regards as trivial (6.125.5). Herodotus also apparently approves of the Alcmaeonids for making a conspicuous show of wealth by refinishing the porch of the temple of Apollo at Delphi in marble instead of in the limestone specified in their contract (5.62).

In the *Histories,* however, no man is as wealthy as Xerxes and no nation as rich as Persia. Herodotus reveals his fascination with the splendid wealth of Xerxes and with the size, riches, and variety of the Persian empire in two long, lavishly detailed, and painstakingly constructed descriptions of the king's army, first on the march from Susa and then in review on the beach at Doriscus.

Out of Xerxes' procession (7.40–41) Herodotus creates a visual masterpiece relying on symmetry, balance, and subtle variation in detail. If soldiers in front of Xerxes have lances pointing down, those after him must point their lances up, and just as some soldiers have silver instead of gold pomegranates, others, instead of pomegranates, have apples.[9] The whole account leaves the reader with a striking impression of the wealth of the Persian empire, whose line of march covers stades, whose men number in the tens of thousands, and whose spears, in a detail that corroborates and confirms the splendor of the Persian army, have ornaments of precious metal.

This account of Xerxes' departure from Sardis, however, forms a mere prelude to the mustering of the whole army at Doriscus, a spectacular tour de force that extends to almost twenty pages in modern editions (7.60–99). Although there are more ornaments of feather and hide than gold and silver, the catalogue shows that the richness of the Persian nation lies not only in precious metals but in the diversity of its people and the gigantic number of races who muster to Xerxes' call.[10]

What is missing from all this description, however, is any note of disapproval of Xerxes' extravagance or any attempt to create a mood of threat or menace. Herodotus emphasizes, rather, the pathos of the scene.[11]

Xerxes' army makes a splendid show, but the reader knows that the Persian troops are doomed. Dire omens strengthen this feeling of tragic irony, and these occur in the passages that precede and follow the two catalogues: an eclipse darkens the departure from Sardis (7.37), lightning bolts and whirlwinds strike unexpectedly (7.42), an unexplained panic (φόβος) sweeps over the men in their camp at Ilium (7.43), and once the army reaches the European side of the Hellespont, two prodigies—both grotesque births—are reported (7.57). In this part of the narrative Xerxes appears in a sympathetic light. The king stops to admire a beautiful plane tree and decorates it with gifts of gold and silver (7.31),[12] a scene that foreshadows his later pleasure in the spectacle of his massed armies. On that occasion, a scene that occurs between the two army catalogues, Herodotus describes the sensitive and emotional reaction of Xerxes to the sight of his gathered forces: the king weeps as he reflects that none of his army will be alive in one hundred years (7.45–46).[13] But the reader, who can see more clearly than the king, feels sorrow for a more immediate tragedy: after only one year, not one hundred, many of these men will not return from Greece alive. Xerxes finds comfort for the transient nature of life in the glorious array of his army, and the reader, Herodotus expects, may share this feeling, too. Although Herodotus exaggerates the size of Xerxes' army partly to enhance the eventual Greek victory, that purpose yields here to unmistakable admiration for the dazzling magnificence of Persia's undertaking. The splendor of Xerxes' army is vain and evanescent, but it is splendid all the same.[14]

We see the danger and limitations of the wealth of prosperous aggressors most often reflected in the moral superiority that poverty has conferred on Herodotus' noble savages. The motif of the noble savage can be traced back in Greek literature to Homer's references to the Ethiopians as "blameless" and "dwelling at the ends of the earth" (*Iliad* 1.423; *Odyssey* 1.22–23) and to the Abii, "drinkers of milk, the most righteous of men" (*Iliad* 13.6); it also supplies one side of Homer's portrait of the Cyclopes.[15] Although Polyphemus is an evil monster who eats human flesh, he and the other Cyclopes share an idyllic, independent, pastoral existence, with a diet normally restricted to milk and cheese. Herodotus' noble savages in general follow the Homeric pattern of remote habitation, simple and rugged lives, restricted diet, and moral rectitude. They inhabit a type of utopia that anthropologists label "hard primitivism" to differentiate this kind of life from its opposite, in

which men like the Phaeacians of the *Odyssey* live at ease in a
paradise where fruit drops from the trees and no one needs to
work.[16]

Herodotus does not, moreover, subscribe to "chronological primitivism" in which a utopia, such as Hesiod's golden
age, is imagined to have existed long ago. There is scarcely a
trace in the *Histories* of belief in a golden age of material plenty,
and Herodotus makes clear his doubt in the existence of the
Hyperboreans (4.36), whose soft lives were proverbial by the
fifth century.[17] Herodotus, rather, represents his rugged primitives as the contemporaries of more advanced civilizations.
Most of his noble savages conform in most of their attributes to
standard examples of the type in world literature. Herodotus'
concept of the noble savage owes something to previous literature, to actual observation, and to his own romantic imagination and that of his informants. But his composite portrait of
the noble savage emphasizes some features more than others
and adds unique characteristics.

At this point it will be helpful to include a brief catalogue, first, of the traits of Herodotus' noble savages and, second, of the types of transactions and experiences—for example,
"exchanges of gifts" or "crossing of boundaries"—that characterize the hostile relationships between noble savages and their
aggressors. These characteristic traits and interactions form a
pattern illustrated by repeated anecdotes, but Herodotus emphasizes different features in different cases. Thus the writer
exercises conscious choice for artistic purposes, and the anecdotes, as we shall see, are not stereotypic repetitions of the
same motifs.

Just as structuralist doctrine emphasizes the anthropological insights possible from a study of diet, so their
eating habits are of first importance to understanding Herodotus' noble savages. They eat raw and unprocessed foods and
drink milk or water rather than wine, which because it must be
"cooked" by fermentation represents higher civilization. When
noble savages do taste wine, they are especially susceptible to
its temptations and bad effects. In technology the noble savages
are predictably simple and at a lower stage of human progress

than the prosperous aggressors. They know and possess gold, often in great quantities, but they have no iron. Paradoxically, because they have gold, they are "rich," but since for them gold is a common, everyday metal to which they attach no special worth, they are also poor. Noble savages have a special liking for horses, and when it comes to battle, their preferred weapon is the bow and arrow. Herodotus particularly stresses the boundaries, *nomoi*—usually rivers or other bodies of water— that enclose and protect the savages from the temptations and delights of the higher civilizations that surround them.

Noble savages have a social organization resembling a utopia, especially as regards their treatment of their children, wives, and elderly. Herodotus portrays in a favorable light not only these social customs but also the laissez-faire, minimalist political structure of primitive societies. His noble savages are innocent, not ignorant. Their religion and ethics are marked by simplicity and directness. They worship few gods or only one, but their worship is honest and deep. Their moral code is simple too, its primary tenet complete reverence for truth. The most obvious contrast between nature and culture is that between hard and soft, strong and weak, but Herodotus' noble savages are more noted for their moral strength than for their physical hardiness. By stressing ethical rather than physical characteristics, Herodotus avoids some of the crudeness and oversimplifications of the Hippocratic essay on "Airs, Waters, and Places," even though he is commonly supposed to rely on doctrines found there. The moral toughness of Herodotus' noble savages expresses itself just as much in words as in actions. These men speak few words, but what they say is worth hearing. Noble savages are intelligent and perceptive in their dealings with prosperous aggressors, whose duplicity they instantly recognize. Their responses are often not only wise but witty. On occasion noble savages choose not to speak at all but to communicate by symbols—gestures or objects given or shown— and here, too, wit can govern their choice.

When noble savages and prosperous aggressors come into contact with one another, certain themes repeatedly characterize their encounters. Boundaries naturally play a key role, since the aggressor must cross a boundary in order to attack the savage. Since the aggressor is ignorant about the nature of the people he is attacking, he characteristically turns to a wise adviser for help. It is in conversations between the aggressor-king and his adviser that we usually first learn in detail the particular traits of the noble savage. Such scenes may take place before or after the crossing of the boundary; there may be several such scenes in one episode of aggression; or the king of the noble savages himself may act as a wise adviser to his attacker. In addition, either before or after crossing the boundary, the prosperous aggressor sends gifts, and usually they are duplicitous gifts, in order to win over his adversary. Often there is an exchange of gifts or messages between the prosperous aggressor and the noble savage. The gift of the noble savage often contains a symbolic, unspoken lesson to his aggressor, and sometimes the reverse pattern is true. It is in this exchange of messages or gifts that we see the savage's wit and we can measure his natural intelligence against the stupidity of his civilized aggressor. These encounters demonstrate the simple, tough virtues of the savage that have been previously catalogued by various wise advisers. The superior virtues of the savages dictate the outcome, for—with one interesting exception to be dealt with later—the savage always wins and defeats his aggressor, whether in debate or on the battlefield; the aggressor retreats back over the savage's protective boundary, distressed by his loss, but—an interesting point—no wiser for his suffering.

   The noble savages of whose lives we hear the most in the *Histories* are the Massagetae, the Ethiopians, and the Scythians, though many tribes Herodotus mentions only briefly belong to the type, and some of their distinctive features or customs contribute to or reinforce the composite portrait. Ironically and significantly, however, the first substantial description of noble savages that we encounter in the *Histories* is of the Persians, who are eventually to become the epitome of the prosperous aggressor. But before they were conquered by the Lydians, the Persians knew "no luxury [ἁβρόν] nor anything good" (1.71.4).[18] The first and fullest statement of the Persians'

status as noble savages comes in the form of the advice of
Sandanis to Croesus against attacking such a rugged people:

> O king, you are preparing to lead your armies against men who
> wear trousers made of hides and the rest of whose clothing is
> leather besides. The food that they eat is not what they want but
> what they have and the land they inhabit is rough. Moreover,
> they make no use of wine but drink water and have no figs to eat
> or anything else that is good. Suppose that you are victorious,
> what will you get from them? On the other hand, if you are
> defeated, consider how many good things you have to lose.
> Once they get a taste [γευσάμενοι] of our luxuries, we will not
> be able to drive them away.[19] For my part I give thanks to the
> gods for not giving the Persians the idea of leading armies
> against the Lydians. (1.71)

It is not at all clear that Herodotus is historically
correct in depicting the early Persians as uninterested in conquest, poorer, and more primitive than the Lydians. Herodotus
himself portrays the Persians at this period, after their triumph
over the Medes, as so thriving that Croesus, at least, wants
preemptively to curtail their power before it leads to expansion.[20] That Herodotus is our only source for the Persians'
leather clothing adds to our suspicions that he is romantically
exaggerating their backwardness to make them conform more
clearly to the ideal of the noble savage. The Persians' rough
leather clothing expresses both their toughness (in contrast to
the fifth-century Greek conception of their costumes as flowing
robes and trousers of soft materials) and their primitivism.[21]
The Persians' dress implies that they are still at a hunting and
gathering state of human evolution and, in their ignorance of
weaving, can only dress in the skins of the animals they have
killed for food. The Persians eat a meager diet. Because of the
barrenness of their land, they have no luxuries like figs, and, a
key identifying mark of most noble savages, they do not drink
wine.[22] This frugality fosters hardiness and physical and military strength, for Sandanis clearly fears the Persians. On the
other hand, he says, though the Persians would be formidable
opponents *if* they attacked Lydia, they evidently will not con-

template such aggression spontaneously; they are content, in their ignorance of any better place, to live within the boundaries of their own harsh land. The savage Persians are therefore hungry and strong but not intrinsically predatory or prone to overseas conquests, a portrait of them not true to Croesus' fears, to Darius' remarks on their territorial imperative (7.11), or to their later history.[23]

The idea of the Persians' self-sufficiency and contentment with their rugged lot—as long as no direct temptation is placed in their way—seems therefore to come from Herodotus' concept of the noble savage rather than from some actual historical source. Geographical boundaries, hinted at in Sandanis' warning, also play an important role in Herodotus' descriptions of the early Persians and of most of the other noble savages as well. Herodotus repeatedly mentions the Halys as the proper boundary between Persia and Lydia (1.6, 28, 72, 103), and Croesus' crossing of the river Herodotus considers a momentous event and describes it at length (1.75).

Herodotus tells us that the Persians readily adopt foreign customs (1.135), but when he comes to catalogue Persian manners (1.135–140)—even though he describes here a later, wealthy Persia now firmly established as a prosperous aggressor—most native Persian traits appear to be survivals of their earlier lives as noble savages.[24] Herodotus writes that each Persian has many wives and many concubines, a practice that we might be tempted at this point to see as a sign of (imported) luxury; but as later comparisons with other noble savages reveal, it is a mark of primitive utopias. Persian values are simple and resemble a warrior's code. After prowess in battle (τὸ μάχεσθαι) the Persians most highly praise "manly virtue" (ἀνδραγαθίη) and after that the possession of many sons. These sons they educate in three things "only" (μοῦνα) from the ages of five to twenty: "to ride, to shoot the bow, and to tell the truth," ἱππεύειν καὶ τοξεύειν καὶ ἀληθίζεσθαι (1.136). Persian children are cloistered with the women until the age of five so that if they die their fathers will be untroubled by grief. Herodotus expresses his approval of these simple, manly ways: αἰνέω μέν νυν τόνδε τὸν νόμον, "I praise this custom" (1.137).

Herodotus also praises the Persians' judicial system because "neither the king nor anyone else" puts a man to death for one single mistake or crime but first considers whether there may be good deeds to outweigh the criminal's faults (1.137). The Persians believe that the most shameful act is to tell a lie (τὸ ψεύδεσθαι) and after that to owe a debt, for debts lead to falsehoods (1.138.1). Their virtues also include respect for nature. Persians do not urinate or spit or wash their hands in rivers and do not permit others to do so, "for they show great reverence for rivers" (1.138.2). All these details contribute to an idealized picture of the Persians, surely unhistorical and violated in many of its specifics by Persians in the *Histories,* but very much in accord with Herodotus' portrait of other noble savages. The Persian king, for example, often puts blameless and innocent men to death, and Xerxes' mistreatment of the Hellespont (7.35) and Cyrus' punishment of the Gyndes (1.189–190) scarcely shows reverence for nature.

The Persians' transition to the status of prosperous aggressors is, therefore, not entirely consistent or believable as an account of an actual historical change, but it is essential to the thematic structure of the *Histories.* Croesus warns Cyrus not to let the unsophisticated Persian troops (ὑβρισταί . . . ἀχρήματοι) sack Sardis because the rich booty will corrupt them and lead them to plot against the king (1.89). Herodotus may also show a transitional stage from noble savage to prosperous aggressor in the object lesson by which Cyrus convinces the Persians to revolt against the Medes (1.126). He invites a group of Persians to spend a day clearing a thorny tract of land "the size of eighteen or twenty stadia" and then has them return for a second day of feasting "with wine." Cyrus then addresses the Persians: "If you follow my wishes you can have things like this [the day of feasting] and thousands of other benefits besides, but if you do not follow my advice you will have numberless sufferings very like those of yesterday [the labor of clearing thorns]" (1.126.5). Because they are tough, the Persians possess the physical strength and stamina to complete the tasks assigned to them and, because they are primitive and simple, they respond to a concrete demonstration of their predicament rather than to a speech. But on the other hand, the Persians do fall prey to the temptations of the luxuries, including the wine, which they taste on the second day; they vote to join Cyrus in a revolt against the Medes in order to secure more of these amenities. The Persians fall short, then, of the finest of Herodotus' noble savages through their inability to resist the temptations of foreign luxury.

The first completely noble savages whom we meet are the Massagetae, whom Cyrus, now a prosperous aggressor, attacks with such disastrous results (1.204–214). Once again, our first inkling of the character of the noble savages comes from a wise adviser, ironically enough Croesus, who warns Cyrus not to attack them. Croesus, in his cautionary speech, stresses the simple life of the Massagetae, the trivial gain possible from such a poor people, and above all, the great likelihood that such an attack and contact between the two races may give the Massagetae a taste of Persian luxury and lead to disastrous counterattack: "They have no knowledge of Persian luxuries [ἀγαθῶν] and indeed have no knowledge at all of great luxuries" (1.207.6).

The Massagetae also inhabit a country surrounded by a natural boundary, the Araxes river (1.201), which both protects them from outside attack and preserves them from the temptations of foreign luxury. Like the early Persians the Massagetae live contentedly within their own borders and feel that other nations ought to do the same. When Cyrus begins to bridge the Araxes river, the Massagete queen sends him a message: "Rule over your own territory and allow us to rule over ours" (1.206.1). But Tomyris knows that Cyrus aims at conquest and so makes him a curious proposal that will remove the necessity for bridges over the Araxes: the Massagetae will retire three days' march and allow the Persians to ford the stream at leisure for a battle in the Massagete country; or, if the Persians prefer, they should similarly withdraw to allow a battle on Persian soil (1.206.2). Cyrus' Persian counselors recommend allowing Tomyris to cross, but Croesus offers contrary advice of great interest for Croesus' character and for Herodotus' belief in the possibility for change in the relationship between noble savage and prosperous aggressor. Because of his experience in attacking Persia, Croesus' advice takes account of the worst possibilities. Although Croesus does point out that if the Persians win the battle on foreign soil, they will have a headstart for further advance into the Massagete countryside, he lays more stress on the danger to Persia of a Massagete victory on Persian soil. In that case the savages will have no natural boundaries between themselves and Persian luxury.

The wisdom of Croesus' caution becomes even clearer when he reveals the nature of a stratagem by which, after accepting Tomyris' offer to retreat, he believes the Massagetae may be defeated. He intends to give the Massagetae a taste of luxury by laying a feast (δαῖτα) for them of meat and *wine* and bread. Cyrus must then retreat to the river, leaving behind the most expendable part of his army. "Then," says Croesus, "we will have an opportunity to make a display of grand deeds" (1.207.7). If Cyrus does adopt this particular strategy, the Persians will place themselves in double jeopardy if they retreat and allow Tomyris to advance into Persia. If Tomyris wins the battle, she will not only have a headstart into Persia but the deceitful (though in this case unsuccessfully deceitful) banquet will have whetted her troops' appetites for Persian booty.[25]

Cyrus does take Croesus' advice. The Massagetae defeat the small Persian force and catch sight of the feast: "Immediately they reclined and feasted, and when they had their fill of wine and food they slept" (1.211). Though the plan does not ultimately succeed, Croesus cannot be blamed. He could not have predicted that when the Persians overwhelm the drunken Massagetae, Sargapises, the son of Tomyris, would be among those taken, that he would commit suicide in remorse, and that Tomyris' vengeful fury would end in the Persians' defeat and Cyrus' death. But otherwise Croesus' advice about crossing the river proves wise, despite Cambyses' later drunken recriminations (3.36), and it has important and enduring consequences both for the defeated aggressors and for the conquering savages. If Cyrus had allowed Tomyris to cross the Araxes, both losers and winners would have fared worse. Although the Persians are defeated in battle, the barrier of the Araxes discourages the Massagetae from further conquest, and Cambyses peacefully takes over his father's throne. The Persians are thus spared the fate of the Lydians—total defeat by a more primitive and warlike race—and the Massagetae escape corruption from the Persian luxuries won by their conquest. Croesus' trick makes Tomyris' taste of luxury bitter instead of sweet and discourages her from seeking more. Being a noble savage, she is ignorant of wine and can only define it awkwardly: "This fruit of the vine that you Persians fill yourselves up with and then go mad so that when the wine reaches your bodies evil words boil up in you . . . this kind of drug [τοιούτῳ φαρμάκῳ] with which you have tricked and entrapped my son . . . !" (1.212.2).

Earlier we saw how Tomyris' eloquence, intelligence, and wit reflected her status as a clever, vengeful queen, but many of Herodotus' noble savages, like Tomyris, also possess these qualities. Tomyris threatens Cyrus: "I swear by the sun, the lord [δεσπότην] of the Massagetae, that however unquenchable your thirst, I will give you your fill of blood" (1.212.3). When he is dead, she dips his head in a skinful of blood and remarks with witty though grisly exactitude that she has fulfilled her vow: "Now I will give you your fill of blood" (1.214.5).

Herodotus closes his account of the Massagete victory with a brief but significant catalogue of their customs: "They have both horsemen and footsoldiers, bowmen and swordsmen. They possess no silver or iron but have abundant bronze and gold. The former they use for swords, arrowheads, and battle-axes and the latter for helmets, belts, and chest bands" (1.215). Each man weds one wife but all women are held in common. A man who wishes a woman simply hangs his quiver on her wagon and consorts with her "without fear," ἀδεῶς (1.216.1). When a man gets old his clan gathers, sacrifices him, boils his flesh with the meat of other animals, and feasts. This end of life the Massagetae regard as the most fortunate (ὀλβιώτατα), but they consider a death from illness a calamity (συμφορήν), for the custom then is to bury, not to sacrifice, the member of the tribe (1.216.2–3). They sow no crops but eat the birds and fish that the Araxes abundantly provides. They drink milk. They worship only the sun, to whom they sacrifice horses, for, as they reason, the swiftest of mortal things should be sacrificed to the swiftest of gods (1.216.4).

Metallurgy (they use bronze, not iron) and diet (they drink milk, not wine, and eat meat instead of bread) mark the Massagetae as primitives. Like most of Herodotus' noble savages, at least some of the Massagetae are mounted bowmen. Their sexual customs, just as those of the Persians, suggest the fulfillment of male fantasies of promiscuous access to women and, like the Agathyrsi, who have their wives in common "so that all men may be brothers" (4.104), the achievement of a social utopia.[26] The land they inhabit appears less harsh than primitive Persia (the bounty of the Araxes suggesting also "soft" primitivism), but their lives are equally simple and warlike, as the triumph over Cyrus shows. Their treatment of their elderly also strikes a utopian note. Herodotus does not explicitly praise this custom, but the language he uses (ὀλβιώτατα, συμφορήν) echoes the stories Solon tells Croesus. This is not a cruel, "barbarian" custom but an economical solution to a social problem. For the Massagetae it is ὀλβιώτατα to die (like Tellus, Cleobis, and Biton) in full possession of one's faculties and συμφορήν to prolong the enjoyment of life to its natural end. The Massagetae, in sum, appear as the purest of Herodotus' noble savages, for after Cyrus, no other nation even attempts to conquer them, and they show no interest in foreign conquest either.[27]

The Nubian Ethiopians (3.18–25), like the Massagetae, live simple, healthy, and long lives, remote from other men. We meet them, like the Massagetae, in the context of an attempt by a prosperous aggressor, Cambyses, to annex their territory. Here, too, the aggressor must advance across natural barriers, the Libyan desert and the Nile. Cambyses mounts his campaign by the ploy of sending gifts—purple cloth, gold necklaces and bracelets, myrrh, and wine (3.20)—just as Cyrus had first approached Tomyris with an offer of marriage (1.205). Cyrus' offer was deceitful and so are Cambyses' gifts, for he sends them in the hands of certain Fisheaters, who are to act as intermediaries but also as spies. Like Tomyris, the Ethiopian king shrewdly sees through the aggressor's tokens of friendship; also like her he scolds the Persian king for wanting territory "other than his own," ἄλλης ἢ τῆς ἑωυτοῦ (3.21.2). Not only does he perceive the insincerity of Cambyses' gesture, he calls the gifts themselves—dyed cloth and myrrh—"deceitful," δολερά (3.22.1, 3), for the dye disguises real colors and the perfume true smells. A society based upon the enjoyment of luxury is thus intrinsically corrupt from the point of view of the noble savage. With a mixture of naiveté, disdain, and shrewdness, the savage king calls the Persian jewelry "fetters," πέδαι (3.22.2), a doubly clever perception since the Persians are enslaved by luxury and the gifts are intended to lure the Ethiopians into slavery to Persia.

The Ethiopians have very little bronze but so much gold that they do not consider it precious (3.23.4). The Ethiopians are thus at an earlier stage of development than the Massagetae, who use bronze freely but not iron. Since the Ethiopians do not recognize luxuries, their lives are "poor" even in their possession of a metal that other nations consider precious. They also possess certain amenities associated with "soft" primitivism: a fountain of youth (3.23.2) and a mysterious "table of the sun," which supplies the people automatically with their diet of boiled meat (3.18). Although, like the Massagetae, the Ethiopians do not have bread and drink only milk (23.1), wine makes a favorable impression on the Ethiopian king—although only in comparison with Persian bread.[28] He enjoys tasting the drink Cambyses has sent and comments: "I don't wonder the Persians live such short lives on a diet of dung [his understanding of bread], but they wouldn't live even that long if it weren't for this drink" (3.22.4). The Ethiopian king sends back to Cambyses a prodigious bow, his own meaningful gift, which symbolizes the Ethiopians' warlike strength, together with the enjoinder: "The king of the Ethiopians advises the king of the Persians that only when the Persians can easily draw a bow of this size should they think of attacking the long-lived Ethiopians with overwhelming forces, but until that time they should give thanks to the gods that they do not give the sons of the Ethiopians the idea of acquiring land in addition to their own" (3.21.3). Here the Ethiopian king acts the part of the wise adviser by warning a prosperous aggressor (Cambyses) not to attack a noble savage. His words recall those with which Sandanis warned Croesus ("give thanks to the gods") against attacking the Persians.

But the similarities in wording point also to some significant differences between the Persians and the Ethiopians. Croesus actually does attack the Persians, who therefore get the idea of counterattacking and adding *his* territory to theirs. Cambyses, on the other hand, has to abandon his expedition because of the lack of enough supplies to reach "the ends of the earth," ἔσχατα γῆς (3.25). The Ethiopians, then, unlike the Persians but like the Massagetae, can and do live on in brave, noble tranquillity. The pure mode of life of these savages, resistant to the temptations of luxury, is a reproach to the Persians for their unwise choice in wishing to rule others rather than to maintain their isolation.

With the Nubian Ethiopians, however, Herodotus faces an embarrassing contradiction. If these Ethiopians remain unconquered, who are the Ethiopian troops whom Herodotus lists in the armies of both Darius and Xerxes (7.69; 9.32)? Herodotus might have eliminated the discrepancy by omitting Ethiopians from the Persian muster list, but apparently their participation was too well known for him to do so. He extricates himself from this difficulty by later implying that Cambyses did conquer *some* Ethiopians but only those who are the closest neighbors of the Egyptians (3.97). Herodotus, then, is willing to leave the reader with some sense of inconsistency in order to maintain his earliest portrait of the Ethiopians as a people totally free and unconquered.[29]

In portraying the Scythians as noble savages, however, Herodotus has to deal with people much better known to his audience than the Ethiopians or Massagetae, particularly at Athens. There, after the Persian wars, Scythian archers—slaves of the state—served as police and as the butt of jokes on the comic stage.[30] In addition, since Greeks traded regularly with the Scyths in the fifth century, they could hardly be said to occupy "the ends of the earth." It was not possible, for example, to allege that the Scythians were ignorant of wine, since it appears to have been common knowledge that Cleomenes had acquired a taste for strong drink from the Scythians (6.84, cf. 4.66). But so vast is the area of Scythia and so varied the tribes that live there that Herodotus, nevertheless, has considerable scope for selection and invention, particularly since he portrays the Scythians at a period prior to regular contact with the Greeks. The Scythians also appeal to Herodotus for certain unique qualities, although they lack some characteristic attributes of other noble savages.

Scythian customs are more patently "barbaric" (in the usual modern meaning) than those of the early Persians, Massagetae, or Ethiopians. Rather than criticize this savagery, Herodotus describes with great interest the most bloodthirsty and ghoulish of the Scythian customs: how they slaughter all their captives, drink thier blood, take scalps and wear them proudly on their saddles, and make drinking cups of the skulls of their vanquished foes (4.64). Only Tomyris dipping Cyrus' severed head into a skinful of blood can compare with the Scythians for Grand Guignol effect. We should also note that blood is a raw, unprocessed substance and thus a suitable beverage for a noble savage. Herodotus presents the Scythians' nomadic life as a fancy-free ideal of independence from authority. Because the Scythians live in wagons, they have no permanent habitations or communities and can easily evade attack by moving (4.46). The dwellers around the Prasias also live unconventionally in huts built on stilts in the lake (5.16), which protects them from the attack of Megabazus and allows them to live an independent, untrammeled life.

Like other noble savages the Scythians are horsemen and, being nomads, plant no crops. They drink milk and disdain the customs of others (4.76). The Scythians are attacked by and eventually defeat a prosperous aggressor, Darius, who advances against them by means of bridges over the Ister, the natural boundary of their territory. A wise adviser, Coes the Lesbian, urges Darius to be careful because Scythia has "no ploughed land and no settled cities" (4.97). Artabanus, who is later to speak out against Xerxes' expedition to Greece, also advises against attacking the Scythians (4.83). The Scythians are not only fierce and warlike but clever, for they, in a "scorched earth" stratagem, force Darius to pursue them over devastated country too ruined to feed his troops. The frustrated Darius sends a message begging that the Scythians either stand and fight or give earth and water as a token of submission. The Scythian king, Idanthyrsus, in his reply, sums up the Scythians' courage and way of life: "This is my way [οὕτω τὸ ἐμὸν ἔχει] O Persian. I have never fled in fear from any man and I do not flee from you now. I am doing nothing new or different from what I have been accustomed to do in peacetime. I will explain to you why I do not join in battle with you now. We have neither cities nor cultivated land for which we might be willing to fight with you, fearing that they might be taken or ravaged" (4.127.2).

Here Idanthyrsus takes the part of the wise adviser and describes the peculiarities of the Scythian race in much the same way as Sandanis and Croesus summarize the characteristic traits of the Persians and the Massagetae. This information, however, he may plausibly give since it is not directly useful to Darius in conquering Scythia. But Idanthyrsus' next words clearly reveal to Darius how to provoke the Scythians into a fight: disturb the tombs of their ancestors. In joining the motif of the wise adviser to that of the noble savage, Herodotus has become momentarily confused. Yet the confusion lays bare how he thinks. It was appropriate that Croesus should both warn and advise, giving positive and negative advice to Cyrus, the prosperous aggressor, about attacking Tomyris the noble savage. Herodotus closely associates Idanthyrsus with Croesus and other helpful advisers because he plays partly the same role in warning a prosperous aggressor not to attack a noble savage. But this similarity tricks Herodotus into letting Idanthyrsus inappropriately assume the second part of Croesus' role as a helpful adviser. Although the Ethiopian king also followed Croesus in giving positive advice about when to attack the Ethiopians ("when you can easily draw a bow like this one," that is, never), the words were tongue-in-cheek and did not disturb the logic of the narrative as Idanthyrsus' words do here.

The beginning of Idanthyrsus' speech also brings into focus an important subsidiary theme of the relationship between Herodotus' noble savages and his prosperous aggressors: their ignorance of one another. Croesus, Cyrus, Cambyses, and Darius have no knowledge at all of the nature of the peoples they are attacking. The Ethiopian king is also typically ignorant of Persian customs. For what, he must ask, do the Persians use bracelets and necklaces? Mutual lack of knowledge particularly characterizes the relationship between the Asian empires and the Greeks, and Idanthyrsus' words thus anticipate Herodotus' picture of the Greeks as noble savages facing Xerxes as prosperous aggressor. Croesus sets the pattern. When the Delphic oracle recommends that he ally himself with "the most powerful of the Greeks," he must inquire who they are and knows nothing about the Athenians or Spartans (1.56). Much later, the Spartans send a brusque warning to Darius not to harm the Ionians, "for we will not permit it" (1.152), a message whose peremptory tone reveals the Spartans' naive underestimation of the Persians' power. Darius' response reveals in turn his own ignorance: "Who are the Spartans?" (1.153). Darius has to have a slave remind him three times nightly during dinner of the name of the Greek city that has caused him such embarrassment: "Sire, remember the Athenians" (5.105). Xerxes, moreover, reveals an even more ominous ignorance of Greek values, for he is surprised to learn that the prize at Olympia is only an olive wreath (8.26). On the Greek side Cleomenes is prepared to set off to conquer Persia until he learns by chance—and is dumbfounded by the information—that Susa is three months' journey from the sea (5.50).

Idanthyrsus' words also contain a specific foreshadowing of the appearance of the Spartans at Thermopylae as noble savages. Darius does not understand why the Scythians will not stand and fight but keep retreating. Idanthyrsus explains that what he does is only "what I have been accustomed to do." The situation of Xerxes facing the Spartans before Thermopylae supplies an exact parallel. Xerxes cannot understand why the Spartans are combing their hair and not running away (7.209).[31] Demaratus explains: "It is a custom with them when they are about to risk their lives to arrange their hair" (7.209.3). But Idanthyrsus' words are not literally true, for although the Scythian custom is always to be on the move, their retreat before Darius is a plan to which they have deliberately resorted. Because many of their fellow Scythians and potential allies have not come to their aid, they resolve not "to fight a straightforward battle," ἰθυμαχίην (4.120, cf. 125.2). But Herodotus forgets this inconsistency because he is dwelling on the Scythians' similarities to other noble savages.

The rest of Idanthyrsus' speech offers further clear parallels in tone and even language to speeches by other noble savages: "As my masters [δεσπότας]," Idanthyrsus proclaims, "I acknowledge only Zeus, my ancestor, and Histria, queen of the Scyths. Instead of earth and water I will send you gifts which are appropriate for you to receive, and as for your saying *you* are my master, you will regret it" (4.127). The Scythians are thus slightly less free and so less simple than the Massagetae, who worship only a single god, the sun, as their δεσπότην (1.212.3). The gifts Idanthyrsus promises to send recall the gift of the king of the Ethiopians and similarly convey a threat to the aggressor (3.21). The Scythians send Darius a bird, a mouse, a frog, and five arrows (4.131), which the Persians at first mistakenly interpret as a gesture of surrender comparable to the sending of earth and water. Gobryas, however, eventually gives the correct interpretation: "Unless you become birds and fly up to the sky or mice and crawl under the earth or frogs and jump into the lakes, you will not escape being pierced by our arrows" (4.132.3). The message thus turns out to be a threat very much like that Tomyris sent to Cyrus ("I will give you your fill of blood"). This wordless message is both primitive, because the Scythians have no system of writing, and sophisticated, because the message shows that the Scythians are more clever than the Persians, who have great difficulty in decoding the meaning of this symbolic message.

When the Persians beg for an interpretation, the Scythians reply with a taunt: "If you are wise [σοφοί], you will figure out for yourselves what the gifts mean" (4.131.2).

When Darius finally does get the Scythians to face him in battle, he receives another concrete illustration of the hopelessness of his cause. At the moment of battle, a rabbit starts up in the no-man's-land between the two armies and the Scythians set off in clamorous pursuit. Darius and the Persians are utterly forgotten (4.134). The Scythians relish triumph over a rabbit more than victory over Persia just as the Ethiopians value their prowess with a bow more than Persian luxury. Darius' retreat back to the Ister proves costly, and the Scythians carry out the threat conveyed by the gifts just as Tomyris carried out hers.

The expedition of Xerxes against Greece follows the general pattern and includes some of the specific motifs of earlier attacks of prosperous aggressors on noble savages. The general similarities are the following: A prosperous king crosses a body of water to attack a people vastly inferior to his own in material goods. The king ignores the warnings of a wise adviser that the people he is attacking possess certain moral and physical qualities, inherent in their poverty, that will make them formidable opponents. The noble savage ultimately defeats the prosperous aggressor to fulfill the adviser's prophecy.

Demaratus plays a part that combines the roles of the kings of the Massagetae, Ethiopians, and Scythians and those of the wise advisers Sandanis, Croesus, and Coes. Demaratus is both a king of noble savages (the Spartans), and hence able to interpret their virtues for Xerxes, and because of his exile, a member of Xerxes' court and sympathetic to the king's cause. Demaratus' words are often quoted, but they bear reexamination in light of the motif of the noble savage: "In Hellas from time immemorial poverty [πενίη] has been a lifelong companion and courage an ally, attained through wisdom and reinforced by the discipline of law. By means of courage Hellas wards off both want and despotism" (7.102). Demaratus' words win the reader's attention and conviction not only through their lapidary simplicity but through echoes of the association between poverty and bravery in the motif of the noble savage. Demaratus goes on to outline the superior virtues of the Spartans in words that conjure up the virtues of other noble savages. When Demaratus says (7.104) that the Spartans serve "law" (νόμος) as their "master" (δεσπότης) we are reminded of the words of Tomyris and the Egyptian king acknowledging only "the sun" or "Zeus and Histria" as their masters. But the Spartans obey a more remote, powerful, and austere master than any of the other noble savages.

Of the Spartans' frugal diet, always an important aspect of the lives of noble savages, we learn indirectly but memorably from the anecdote of the "two feasts of Pausanias" (9.82). After the battle of Plataea the victorious Spartan general, who has captured the Persian bakers (ἀρτοκόπους) and chefs (ὀψοποιούς), has them prepare a feast "just as they did for Mardonius," using the "gold and silver service [παρασκευήν] and multicolored hangings" that the retreating Persians had left behind. Then he has his own attendants (διηκόνους) prepare a "Laconian feast." Pausanias calls the Greek generals together and addresses them: "Hellenes, I have gathered you here because I want to show you the foolishness of the Persians, who have meals like this [τοιήνδε δίαιταν] but who came to deprive us of such penurious fare as we have here." Herodotus does not actually describe the Spartan meal, but the implied contrast conjures up meager fare.

Pausanias, who has the two meals prepared "as a joke" (ἐπὶ γελῶτι), in this way gives an example of Spartan wit and of the Spartan preference for wordless demonstrations over speeches and for few words over many. When the Samian exiles, to take another example, try with long speeches to persuade the Spartans to send aid against Polycrates, the Spartans claim to have forgotten the beginning of these speeches by the end. The Ionians, perhaps annoyed at this slight to their eloquence and wishing to make an answering sally against the Spartans' obtuseness, bring out an empty sack and announce: "This sack needs grain." Won over by the directness and simplicity of this appeal, the Spartans agree to help; but they still indicate their preference for messages without words, complaining that the Ionians needed only to show the empty sack and say nothing (3.46).[32]

When Spartans do speak, their words are few and to the point. Before the battle of Thermopylae, when the Spartan Dieneces hears that the Persian army is so numerous that their arrows will darken the sun, he wryly remarks: "It would be a good thing because then they could fight in the shade" (7.226.2). Dieneces' gruff words serve as a suitable introduction to the three Simonidean epitaphs for the dead at Thermopylae. The second of these, the most famous, couched in terms of a Spartan message, perfectly expresses the noble savage's habitual understatement and brevity of speech. Here is Rawlinson's eloquent translation:

> Go stranger, to Lacedaemon tell
> that here, obeying her behest, we fell.
>
> (7.228)

We learn generally of the toughness of noble savages from wise advisers who describe their dress and style of life and caution against attacking them. Herodotus also presents an ethnographic *logos* on the Spartans (6.56ff.) that recalls those for other noble savages, but there is no description of the Spartan fighting kit to compare with Sandanis' description of the Persians' leather trousers. But since Spartan equipment was well known to Herodotus' readers, he can refer to it indirectly by allusion and contrast as he does in Aristagoras' request to Cleomenes to help the Ionian revolt by attacking Persia (5.49). Herodotus here reverses the normal situation of a wise adviser warning a prosperous aggressor not to attack noble savages because they dress roughly, fight fiercely, eat meager fare, and live in a poor land whose conquest will not benefit the conqueror. Aristagoras is a foolish adviser recommending to a noble savage to attack a prosperous aggressor because victory will be easy and the benefits obvious:

> This will be easy for you to do for the barbarians are not warlike, and you have acquired the greatest proficiency in war. Their

manner of fighting is with the bow and the short sword. Trousers [ἀναξυρίδας] are what they wear into battle and turbans on their head so they will be easily conquered. They have luxuries [ἀγαθά] in their land such as no one else possesses, starting with gold, silver, bronze, embroidered raiment, oxen and slaves, all the things you could have to your heart's content if you wanted to. (5.49.3–4)

Aristagoras' words imply a contrast with Spartan spears, long swords, and bronze helmets. The Spartan Cleomenes feels tempted by this prospect of easy conquest, for he asks for a delay of three days in which to make a decision. But as a noble savage Cleomenes must refuse the temptation to become a prosperous aggressor. Refuse he does, but not for honorable motives, only because of the long distance involved.

Not all Greeks are as noble as the Spartans, and not all Spartans are equally incorruptible. The Greeks in general most closely resemble, among the noble savages, the Scythians, who comprise many tribes of differing habits and unequal bravery in the face of an invader from abroad. When the Scythians canvass their allies for aid against Darius, Herodotus anticipates the same action by Athens and Sparta with the same mixed success before the invasion by Xerxes. We see the bravery of the few reflected in the cowardice of the many. The Greeks generally and the Spartans in particular fall short of the perfect ideal of the noble savage. The Spartans, for example, have aggressive tendencies, of which Aristagoras complains to Cleomenes: "You insist on warring against your rivals the Messenians as well as the Arcadians and Argives, who have territory which is not so large and with limited boundaries and have neither gold nor silver that might prompt one to fight and die out of a desire to possess it" (5.49.8). In fact, we first meet the Spartans (1.66) as relatively prosperous aggressors against the Arcadians and Tegeans. Like Croesus, whose fate their own experience foreshadows, the Spartans crave the land of their neighbors and consult the Delphic oracle. In its response the oracle plays the role that Sandanis is soon to fill in advising Croesus not to attack the leather-trousered, water-drinking Persians: "You ask for Arcadia? It is a great thing you ask of me. I will not grant it to you. In Arcadia there are many men who eat acorns [βαλ-ανηφάγοι] and they will prevent you" (1.66). The Spartans may be savages relative to Xerxes and they may be tough and brave, but they stand no chance of defeating men who eat acorns. Indeed, they prove no match even for the Tegeans, whom the oracle slyly lures them into attacking as an alternative.

Herodotus' story of Scythians and Amazons (4.110–116), even though it violates the noble savage–prosperous aggressor motif in some aspects, provides important evidence of the subtlety with which he weighs the contradictory claims of nature and culture. In the course of recounting Darius' unsuccessful campaign against the Scythians, Herodotus digresses on the customs of the local natives. Within this digression he devotes several pages to the customs of the Sauromatae, a remote Scythian tribe whose women ride with the men both to hunt and to battle. Herodotus then explains the warlike demeanor of these Sauromatian women with a lively etiological story of intermarriage in remote antiquity between a group of Scythians and a band of fugitive Amazons.

Some Amazons, after having been captured at the battle of Thermodon and while being transported aboard three ships, rose up and killed their captors. With no knowledge of ships or navigation, the women drift at the whim of "wave and wind" (κατὰ κῦμα καὶ ἄνεμον [4.110.2]) until they come to Scythian territory on the shores of Lake Maeotis. The Amazons quickly rustle horses and plunder the countryside. When in the course of defending their land the Scythians learn their attackers are women, they cease hostilities and dispatch a band of their own young men to camp as closely as possible to the Amazons and befriend them. After a period of gradually increasing fraternization, the Amazons and Scythian young men set up rough housekeeping together. The young men then propose marriage, but the Amazons pronounce themselves unable to adapt to the Scythians' mores. Instead, the newly formed small alliance of Amazons and Scythians retreats three days' journey beyond the river Tanais, "the land they inhabit now" (τὸν χῶρον ἐν τῷ νῦν κατοίκηνται [4.116.1]). And so, says

Herodotus, the present warlike Sauromatian women owe their customs to their ancient Amazon great-grandmothers.

This charming, happily-ever-after tale seems not only remote from Herodotus' main theme—the conflict between Greece and Persia—but a perfect example of his alleged gullibility and willingness to detour from the main course of his narrative to tell *any* amusing story, no matter how irrelevant. The sources of the story's appeal for both modern and ancient audiences are easy to suggest. We relish the boy-girl romance, so rare in classical Greek literature, as well as the Peter Pan theme of young people forming their own culture (beyond the Tanais), away from the responsibilities imposed by parents and adult society. What the modern feminist critic might relish as a story of woman's triumph over man (the Amazons oblige the young Scythians to renounce *their* homes and even to provide "dowries" for the new unions), the ancient male reader probably treated as hilarious exaggeration and comically preposterous role reversal. We need not doubt that Herodotus, too, delights in the story's topsy-turviness and intends through this—as through other, similar stories of human antipodes and bizarre behavior (e.g., 1.196 [the Babylonian "marriage market"], 2.36 [the Egyptians do everything backwards])—some criticism of the strictness of Hellenic customs surrounding the relations between the sexes. Indeed, recent critics such as Hartog, Rossellini, Saïd, and Tyrrell have convincingly shown Herodotus' ability to create in his descriptions of primitive peoples an alternative universe, a mirror utopia of Greek culture. In the background of the Amazon and Scythian story too, of course, lie Greek sophistical attempts to account rationally and non-judgmentally for the diversity of human society and particularly, as Pembroke has shown, for the traces of apparent matriarchy that the Hellenes encountered in some primitive societies.[33]

Nevertheless, despite some attention from feminist and structuralist critics in recent years, I believe that the chief significance of the story of the Scythians and Amazons for the *Histories* and its cleverness have been overlooked. This story repeats many of the themes associated with the prosperous aggressor–noble savage motif, and where it fails to follow or reverses the pattern, the reversal provides insight into Herodotus' attitude to the Persian war and to nature and culture in general. According to my interpretation it is the Amazons who play the role of the noble savages in this story. They steal horses because like many noble savages, such as the early Persians and the Scythians themselves, they have an innate preference for horses as well as for fighting with the bow and arrow. Their plundering of the Scythian territory is not an act of aggression but only their normal mode of life, which they practice in Scythia only because chance has brought them there. The Scythians are thus placed in the position of having to become aggressors against the Amazons in order to protect their territory. Ignorance of the true nature of the Amazons, however, hampers the Scythians: "They were not able to comprehend the matter [οὐκ εἶχον συμβαλέσθαι τὸ πρῆγμα] for they didn't recognize their language, dress, or race" (4.111.1). The Scythians don't even realize at first that the Amazons are *women* and only find out later when they examine the corpses of some fallen in battle.

Herodotus here presents us with an extreme case of the prosperous aggressor's ignorance of his noble-savage adversary. Indeed, if Croesus had truly known the nature of the Persians, Cyrus that of the Massagetae, Cambyses that of the Ethiopians, or Darius that of the Scythians, they never would have considered aggression against a noble savage in the first place. This ignorance of the prosperous aggressor culminates at the end of the *Histories* in the ignorance of Xerxes about the Greeks he is attacking, particularly before Thermopylae when he sees the Spartans combing their hair before the battlements: "He was not able to comprehend the truth [οὐκ εἶχε συμβαλέσθαι τὸ ἐόν] that they were preparing either to kill or be killed" (7.209.1).

Abandoning direct assault, the Scythians dispatch some of their young men to pacify the Amazons by gentler means. These young men constitute a kind of gift, but a gift with an ulterior motive, for the Scythians ultimately want to get, not give: "The Scythians made these plans [ἐβουλεύσαντο] because they planned [βουλόμενοι] to beget children on them" (4.111.2). Most Herodotean prosperous aggressors, we now know, begin their aggression with the offer of a similar duplicitous gift, as Cyrus, for example, begins by offering an alliance by marriage with the Massagete queen Tomyris (1.205), and Cambyses by sending the Ethiopian king purple robes, jewelry, perfume, and wine (3.21). Usually the noble savage, after some hesitation, has the intelligence to reject these false gifts. Similarly, although the Amazons like sex with the Scythians well enough, they ultimately reject the Scythian offer of incorporation into Scythian society. "We could never live with your women," they say, "for our customs are not the same as theirs." Here the Amazons go on to describe their style of life in words that recall the early Persians' education of their sons: "We shoot with bow and arrow, strike with the lance, and ride horseback," ἡμεῖς μὲν τοξεύομέν τε καὶ ἀκοντίζομεν καὶ ἱππαζόμεθα (4.114.3, cf. 1.136).

The Amazons themselves are now placed in the position of having to explain their mores to their attackers. This is the "wise adviser–tragic warner" role played by Sandanis in his advice to Croesus (1.71), but as often as not played also by the noble savage chief. The Amazon speech also illustrates another common trait of noble savages: candor and truthfulness. Initially, however, the Amazons and Scythians are unable to talk to one another because they speak different languages. Instead, the young people communicate by gestures. After a Scythian youth first meets an Amazon alone by chance and has sex with her, she proposes another encounter: "By gestures [χειρί] she proposed that he should come next day to the same place, signaling [σημαίνουσα] that there should be two of them [of the Scythians] and that she too would bring another" (4.113.2). Herodotean noble savages routinely communicate by means of signs or tokens. So Tomyris acts out her threat to satisfy Cyrus' bloodthirstiness by dipping his severed head in a bucket of blood (1.214.5). The Ethiopian king in return for Cambyses' gifts sends an unstringable Ethiopian bow (3.21.3). The noble savage's preference for communication by talismans or tokens when direct speech seems also possible reveals his innocence as well as his charm. Herodotus' Amazons present an extreme case of innocence, because they appear to have had no experience of sex—not even to know what it is, as Tomyris and the Ethiopian king have no conception of wine (1.212.2; 3.21). When the first Scythian youth draws near the first Amazon, Herodotus says, "The Amazon did not push him off but allowed it to happen" (περιεῖδε χρησάσθαι [4.113.1]). We can here note in the Amazon story a further theme often found in descriptions of noble-savage communities: utopianism. The Amazons and young Scythians establish an ideal community in which the number of men and women is equal, there are no old people to be cared for, and no dowries need to be provided for the women.

All these motifs, then—the association with horses and bow and arrow, duplicitous gifts, communication by signs, mutual ignorance, and utopianism—ally this apparently trivial anecdote with the major theme of nature-culture or noble savage–prosperous aggressor in the *Histories.* At this point, however, the anecdote takes a novel turn. Usually, the noble savage lives protected behind some natural barrier. The early Persians lived on the other side of the Halys, the Massagetae beyond the Araxes, the Ethiopians beyond the Libyan desert, the Scythians the Ister, and the Greeks, of course, the Hellespont. But the Amazons and Scythians find themselves *together* in Scythia. The Amazons say they are unable to preserve their noble purity in a culture as refined and decadent as that of the Scythians. So austere is the Amazon code, therefore, that the Amazons find soft the life of a people who take scalps and drink blood from their enemies' skulls. Thus they must retreat beyond the Tanais in order to preserve their mores.

In one other and even more important respect, this story fails to follow the normal pattern of the attack of a prosperous aggressor on a noble savage, for the Amazons, in an event unique in the *Histories,* defeat their prosperous aggressors in both a literal and a metaphorical sense. Cambyses gives up his expedition against the Ethiopians and thus suffers defeat in a literal sense, but he does not view this failure as a lesson that he ought to give up wearing jewelry and drinking wine. According to the pattern that Herodotus has established, the noble savage triumphs over his enemy because of his harsh life and his simple moral code. Then one of two events follows. Either the noble savage lives on, untainted by civilization, behind his natural boundary (as the Massagetae and Ethiopians do), or he falls prey (as the Persians do) to the delight of the attackers' soft life and equally soft morals. The Scythian young men, on the other hand, abandon their relatively higher culture and accept a life harsher but therefore nobler than before in order to share their lives with the Amazons.

In this unique case in the *Histories* then, men of culture deliberately choose nature instead. Is Herodotus saying that such action is desirable or possible? I think not, because for me Herodotus' story of Scythians and Amazons is a clever joke, but a joke concealing a serious point. Herodotus presents the idea of forsaking civilization in such an atmosphere of fairy tale and Never-never-land that it is hard to take the story literally even though we must take it seriously. The real question is how do we apply the lesson of the noble savage and prosperous aggressor in this story to the Greeks after their victory over the Persians? I think the anecdote about the Amazons gives us a clue to Herodotus' thinking: only in fairy tales do noble savages manage not only to preserve their innocence but to convert their aggressors to a simpler and more virtuous life.

At the conclusion of the *Histories* the Greeks, whom Herodotus depicts as noble savages, defeat a prosperous aggressor, the Persians. Yet this final struggle, the culminating example of the motif, not only builds on preceding examples but exceeds them in its complex significance. We have seen how the Scythians most resemble the Greeks because neither group is homogeneous or united in its opposition to the prosperous aggressor. As we have also seen, even the noblest of the Scythians are prosperous aggressors relative to the Amazons. So the Persians stand in the same relationship to the Scythians as the Scythians do to the Amazons. With the Greeks, on the other hand, the antithetical relationship between the Athenians and the Spartans—introduced in the opening chapters of Book One, where we see the former ridden by political factionalism and the

latter by militarism and superstition—adds a fourth and problematic level of complexity. If Persia seeks to conquer Greece,
and Sparta to conquer her Peloponnesian neighbors, whom does
Athens seek to conquer?[34] If the Greeks follow the pattern of
the Scythians, the chain of relationship should be that Persia is to
Greece as Athens is to Sparta as Sparta is to Messenia.

The extent to which Herodotus touches, if at all, on
the coming conflict between Athens and Sparta in the Peloponnesian war is unclear. Here, I feel, in the suggestion of a pattern
that destines Athens to become the prosperous aggressor
against a noble-savage Sparta, Herodotus is either remarkably
prescient or shrewd in his observation of contemporary trends.
The *Histories* does portray the transformation of the Athenians
into prosperous aggressors after the Persian wars, and so the
beginning of Athens' rise to imperial power. But here again
scholars differ on whether Herodotus condemns Athens for
this aggression or speaks as her apologist, defending her past
record of bravery against Persia at a time when her present
drive toward empire was making her unpopular. But the pattern of the motif analyzed here points to an answer. Herodotus
disapproves of tendencies that make Athens resemble the Lydians and the Persians more than the Massagetae and the
Ethiopians.

The Athenians enjoy two triumphs over Persia, the
first led by Miltiades at Marathon and the second ten years later
under Themistocles. The actions of these two Athenian generals after each of these victories, as Herodotus reports these
events, clearly recall in an unkindly light the various barbarian
aggressors encountered earlier in the *Histories*. After Marathon
Miltiades besieges Paros and attempts to extort money from the
islanders by alleging that the Parians contributed a ship to the
Persian forces (6.133–135). Whether or not this accusation is
true and this aggression justified, the outcome shows the gods'
disapproval. A priestess of Nemesis promises to betray the
island to Miltiades; while meeting with this woman behind enemy lines and in the sanctuary at night, Miltiades trips over the
fence of the sacred precinct and injures his leg. The goddess
evidently resents this intrusion, for the wound develops gan-

grene. Ultimately, the Athenian general dies miserably because, as the Pythia pronounces: "Miltiades was fated to end ill" (6.135.3). This sequence of events matches exactly the death of Cambyses: there are acts of profanation (entering the sanctuary of Nemesis; stabbing the bull of Apis [3.33]); a leg injury is ultimately fatal after a lingering illness (scraped knee or dislocated thigh; accidental cut [3.64.3]); and there is a predestined death (prophesied by the oracle of Pythia and the oracle of Buto [3.64.4]).

The case of Themistocles offers even closer parallels to the behavior of the prosperous aggressor. After the final defeat of Xerxes and Mardonius, Themistocles counsels destroying the bridges over the Hellespont to trap the Persians within enemy territory (8.108–109). The discussions of the merits of this maneuver recall the Persian debate about allowing Tomyris to cross the Araxes. Will Mardonius be more dangerous in Europe or if allowed to return unharmed to his own territory? Themistocles clearly favors a counterattack that will totally destroy the Persian army and allow Greece—and himself—to enjoy the booty of the Persian empire. Disappointed in this hope, he undertakes, in a clear imitation of Miltiades, to besiege and extort money from the Greek islanders who had Medized. Here, too, self-interest plays a role. He attacks Andros (8.111), and the details of this act of aggression reveal many of the significant characteristics of the attacks of a prosperous aggressor on a noble savage. Themistocles announces to the Andrians that two great gods, "Persuasion and Necessity" (Πειθώ τε καὶ ᾽Αναγκαίην) require the Andrians to pay the sum demanded. The Andrians reply:

> Of course with good reason Athens is great and prosperous [εὐδαίμονες] and has been successful with the aid of helpful gods. But the Andrians are in the worst possible state as far as the poor quality of their land [γεωπείνας] and have only two unhelpful gods—Poverty and Inability [Πενίην τε καὶ ᾽Αμηχανίην]—who will not leave their island and have even formed a long-standing attachment for the place. These being the gods they have, the Andrians will not pay the money. There will never be a time at

which the power of the Athenians will be stronger than the
Andrians' powerlessness. (8.111.2–3)

The Andrians identify the Athenians as "pros-
perous," and they describe the poverty of their land, a characteristic and significant feature for understanding the primitive
and tough Persians and, ironically, the Greeks. The "poverty,"
which Demaratus calls a "lifelong companion" to Greece as a
whole, the Andrians have elevated to a divinity. Now we see
that relative to the Andrians, the Athenians inhabit a rich land
and thus in this important respect fill the role of a prosperous
aggressor.

The Massagetae worship only one god, the Scythians
two. The Andrians' pantheon is similarly reduced to only two
divinities: poverty and inability. The Andrians' response also
gives an illustration of native wit, for their two gods, like the
two Athenian gods Themistocles mentions, also have names
that begin with the letters pi and alpha. The competition in gods
between Athens and Andros also recalls the competition in gifts
between Cambyses and the Ethiopian king, in which luxurious
trifles are weighed against a simple bow. The Athenian and
Andrian gods, like the Persian and Ethiopian gifts, symbolize
the difference in resources and values between the prosperous
aggressors and the noble savages. Although the Andrians modestly do not mention their toughness and bravery, we may presume it, since the Athenians never do conquer Andros in the
Histories (8.121). Other islands capitulate rather than share the
Andrians' plight.

On balance, however, we cannot say that Herodotus'
respect for noble savages—so often, like the Andrians, morally
in the right—outweighs his admiration for wealth and power.
Although he idealizes the life of the noble savage, Herodotus is
a realist. We can see, in fact, his reservations about primitive
life in the darker side that he shows of two common traits of
primitive people: cannibalism and sexual promiscuity. Although the Massagetae (1.216), Padaeans (3.99), and Issedo-
nians (4.26) eat human flesh, their anthropophagy rises out of
philosophical belief and, by removing the burden of the elderly

and the sick, solves a social problem. The Massagetae and Isse-donians, moreover, make their feast of human flesh more palat-able—or at least less gruesome—by mixing in the flesh of other animals. Elsewhere, however, Herodotus paints a crueler and more realistic picture of cannibalism as a descent to a bestial level. He finds no justification for the exclusively cannibalistic diet of the Androphagoi, for he calls them "the most savage of men, who pay no attention to the laws of Zeus" (4.106).

Finally, in a passage whose true significance has only recently been recognized because of new insights by struc-turalist anthropologists, Herodotus represents the failure of the expedition of Cambyses against Ethiopia as a progressive degra-dation of the king's troops. The soldiers, driven by hunger, deteriorate from men to savage animals and ultimately turn cannibal. When the army has exhausted its supplies of food from Persia, the men slaughter and eat their pack animals, then start to eat grass, and at last turn to "the eating of their own kind," ἀλληλοφαγίην. A horrified Cambyses calls back his troops (3.25).[35]

Sexual promiscuity often appears in a social utopia, for example, in the reason given by the Agathyrsi for sharing their wives: "that all men may be brothers" (4.104). The Mas-sagetae have intercourse with one anothers' wives but show delicacy of feeling and concern for etiquette by hanging their quivers outside the wagons of the women with whom they are consorting in order to avoid awkward encounters with the hus-bands (1.216). The Nasamonians also leave a warning token at such moments (4.172). But Herodotus is also aware of the disquieting implications of total sexual freedom: men can be-come debased to the bestial level. While the Massagetae make love in the privacy of wagons and contrive to avoid embarrass-ing intrusions, the tribes around the Caucasus have intercourse "in the open air just like cattle," ἐμφανέα κατά περ τοῖσι προ-βάτοισι (1.203). Similar are certain Indians for whom sexual intercourse "is in the open just like cattle" ἐμφανής ἐστι κατά περ τῶν προβάτων (3.101). With another tribe, the Ausees, Herodotus not only describes a lack of modesty about sexual intercourse but suggests the absence of stable family structure:

"They have intercourse with their women indiscriminately [ἐπίκοινον], not cohabiting [οὔτε συνοικέοντες] but having sex in the manner of beasts [κτηνηδόν τε μισγόμενοι]. Then the Ausees assign their three-month-old children to the fathers they most resemble" (4.180).[36]

Even the finest and truest of the noble savages live a precarious existence, always, once borders are bridged, susceptible to the temptations of luxury. The integrity even of the Ethiopians rests only on the tenuous prop of the forbearance of their king, who takes a little wine but not enough to color his judgment in rejecting Cambyses' gifts.

In the *Histories* we meet the noble savage and the prosperous aggressor chiefly in exaggerated extremes, the former perfectly brave and hardy, the latter totally effete and enslaved to a luxurious life. The Ionians come closest to occupying a midpoint, geographically as well as culturally, between eastern opulence and Hellenic penury; but although Herodotus praises the climate of Ionia (1.142), its temperateness leads to a way of life that he condemns. The Ionians do not possess enough wealth to be enviable, nor are they poor and tough.[37] In the *Histories,* civilization—represented by wealth—is a beneficial drug, but men either eschew it utterly or take it to excess. In human history, therefore, Herodotus examines the extreme alternation between total prosperity and utter misfortune and the consequences of that change. This theme he announces at the beginning of his work: "I shall treat equally small and great cities of men, knowing that human happiness is never a constant but those cities which formerly were great are now small and those which formerly were small have become great" (1.5). He states this theme even more strikingly in Croesus' advice to Cyrus: "There is a cycle in human affairs which does not allow the same men always to prosper" (1.207). Croesus' words mean, in terms of the motif studied here, that new aggressors, powerful yet enervated by luxury, will forever be encroaching on noble savages, poor yet toughened by their poverty, and will forever be brought low, their place almost inevitably taken by the newly corrupted savages. Thus the *Histories* ends on a warning note: the past has revealed an inevitable cycle for the future.

4

Freedom and Discipline:
Cruel Tyrants and
Philosopher Kings

The *Histories,* according to prevailing opinion, extols freedom and condemns tyranny. "The picture of tyranny and tyrants given by Herodotus," write How and Wells, "is one of almost unrelieved blackness."[1] But this idea arises from a sentimental regard for Athenian democracy as a universal symbol of political freedom rather than from a thorough study of all Herodotus writes or implies about the pros and cons of one-man rule. For Herodotus freedom and one-man rule are extreme opposites that possess parallel and equal merits and defects. Freedom, an enviable condition, can lead to anarchy or can bring the power to enslave others. Servitude, on the other hand, though intrinsically odious, need not preclude and may even foster nobility if men serve a noble master. One-man rule, moreover, though liable to misuse, possesses certain advantages over less authoritarian political systems.

 Herodotus does not distinguish carefully between individual freedom and freedom in international relations, for he believes the two share analogous merits and flaws. Herodotus also does not, for similar reasons, differentiate among tyrants, kings, and despots, whether Greek or barbarian. He uses the words τύραννος, βασιλεύς, and δεσπότης interchangeably.[2] Although he can—to serve a literary purpose—give his stories of eastern kings an oriental flavor, Herodotus treats one-man rule as an institution unaffected by national character. Nor does he see differences between a ruler who has inherited his throne and one who has won his power by force. For Herodotus the interesting question is whether or not a sovereign rules justly once in power.

The famous conversation between Demaratus and Xerxes illustrates Herodotus' contradictory views of democracy and monarchy. Xerxes suggests to Demaratus that the Persian army will conquer the Greeks because the Hellenes are "all alike free and not under the rule of one man," ἐλεύθεροι πάντες ὁμοίως καὶ μὴ ὑπ᾽ ἑνὸς ἀρχόμενοι (7.103.3). But Demaratus defends the bravery of his Lacedaemonian countrymen by describing their synthesis of freedom and discipline: "Though they are free, they are not altogether free, for they have a law which rules them as a despot [ἔπεστι γάρ σφι δεσπότης νόμος]. They fear this law more than your subjects fear you and do exactly what it dictates" (7.104.4). The Spartans will triumph over the Persians because they obey a type of tyrant and are not wholly free. Ironically then, Xerxes fails because his soldiers do not obey him with sufficient servility but need to be whipped and forced into battle by their officers (e.g., 7.56.1; 7.223.3). In this passage Herodotus associates tyranny with good discipline and freedom with sorry disorder. No other people in the *Histories* enjoys such a perfect combination of freedom and discipline as the Spartans, but elsewhere Herodotus does offer significant examples of tyrannies that prove beneficial. These passages show that the anecdote of Demaratus is not an exception to but an illustration of Herodotus' belief in the superiority of the absolute rule of a good master. Though the Spartans serve an abstract ideal, other anecdotes show that Herodotus approves of such flesh and blood tyrants as Deioces and Amasis.

The stories of Deioces, the first king of the Medes (1.96–101), Pisistratus (1.59–64), and Darius (3.73–78, 80–

87) best illustrate this aspect of Herodotus' political thinking.[3] In these passages Herodotus argues for the superiority of tyranny over other forms of government. These passages invite comparison with others—particularly the account of Psammetichus and Amasis in Book Two—that also reveal Herodotus' underlying belief in the merits of one-man rule.

The stories Herodotus tells about the accession of these monarchs to their thrones contain, as we shall see, the same significant motifs. What emerges is a composite portrait of the Herodotean philosopher king, whose benign and beneficial rule demonstrates the superiority of monarchy to other systems of government. This philosopher king contrasts sharply with the cruel tyrant, who plays a memorable role in other parts of the *Histories*. Herodotus thus gives his readers positive exemplars of one-man rule to contrast with negative ones. Of course, he does clearly portray the potential for evil in tyranny—the susceptibility of the ruler to avarice, viciousness, and brutality—and nowhere more effectively than in his portrait of the crazed king Cambyses. What is not recognized, however, is the contrasting picture of the philosopher king, and for this reason I will concentrate on the latter figure in order to establish that Herodotus' attitude to one-man rule is ambivalent and deliberately contradictory. Some of his monarchs are excellent and wise rulers, who bring discipline to their fractious subjects, whereas others are paradigms of savage despotism.

Usually the philosopher king gets his throne by a complex deception, or else, because of his superior intelligence he intuitively and quickly recognizes before any competitor an opportunity for the throne. In either case the philosopher king contrives to give the appearance of his having been drafted by others to rule rather than having actively sought power himself. Ironically, this philosopher king gains power not only by manipulation and trickery but by using (for his own noble ends) some of the very same devices used by the *i*gnoble, cruel tyrants. Because the philosopher king establishes a benevolent rule, he justifies by his actions the principle that the end justifies the means. The philosopher king in Herodotus, in fact, often at first appears—or threatens soon to reveal himself as—a cruel tyrant. His story therefore contains a surprise twist as the reader realizes that this man really *is* good after all.

These rulers usually begin life as commoners with no dynastic claims to the throne, so that once established in power they must try to conceal their humble backgrounds, or else they must explicitly try to justify ruling in spite of their origins. In these stories Herodotus always contrasts the cleverness and wisdom of the philosopher king with the foolishness and gullibility of his subjects, who are easily duped and reveal themselves unable to live peaceably or happily without the authority of an absolute ruler.

When Herodotus discusses the merits of one-man rule, he takes a position likely to be offensive to some of his Greek readers, as we can see from the evil connotations of the word τύραννος in Greek tragedy and from Herodotus' own description of Greek sentiments in favor of political freedom.[4] Herodotus is aware of the potential unpopularity of this position, but he does not temper his narrative to his audience's taste. In the Deioces story Herodotus focuses on aspects of one-man rule liable to have the most repellent associations for his audience and describes them as the strengths instead of the weaknesses of a closed society.

The account of Deioces comes at the beginning of a digression, Herodotus' description of the boyhood and accession of Cyrus, the first king of an independent Persia: "And now I will tell who this Cyrus was and how the Persians came to rule Asia" (1.95.1). The defeat of the Medes brings the Persians to power and Deioces is the first king of the Medes, so Herodotus tells his story before he actually starts to write of Cyrus. But just before he begins the story of Deioces—in words that emphasize the significance of what he intends to write about both Deioces and Cyrus—Herodotus states that his account is "the truth," τὸν ἐόντα λόγον, and that he has rejected "three other versions," τριφασίας ἄλλας λόγων ὁδούς, in favor of this one (1.95.1). Although the stories of Cyrus and Deioces appear at first to be digressions, they introduce the theme of the rise and expansion of Persia and link Book One to the climax of the *Histories:* the defeat of Persia. The story of Deioces runs parallel stylistically to the Gyges story because it, too, is the first illustration of important themes in the *Histories:* here, the author's ideas about the potential of one-man rule to create a stable, just, and happy society. This anecdote merits special attention, too, since commentators so often treat it as "a typical tyrant's progress."[5]

Deioces' story begins with a brief account of the end of the 520-year enslavement of the Medes to the Assyrians. The Medes "fought against the Assyrians for their freedom [ἐλευθερίης], became brave men [ἄνδρες ἀγαθοί], cast off their servitude [τὴν δουλοσύνην], and won their freedom [ἐλευθερώθησαν]." The rest of the Assyrians' subjects, with the example of the Medes before them, also revolted against their masters (1.95.2). Herodotus' choice of words here celebrates the triumph of good (freedom) over evil (servitude). But we learn that this triumph was short-lived: "All on the mainland were now independent [αὐτονόμων] but fell once again into tyranny [ἐς τυραννίδας] in the following manner. There was a clever man [ἀνήρ . . . σοφός] among the Medes whose name was Deioces, the son of Phraortes. This Deioces became consumed with a passion for tyranny [ἐρασθεὶς τυραννίδος] and did as follows" (1.96.1–2). These sentences sketch Deioces' character: a cunning schemer and a subverter of the freedom so bravely won by the Medes. Herodotus uses language—ἐρασθεὶς τυραννίδος— that echoes the fatal infatuation of Candaules—ἠράσθη . . . γυναικός (1.8.1)—and suggests an unscrupulous adventurer, perhaps like Candaules, fated to suffer for his actions.[6]

After this introduction, however, the story takes two sudden and surprising turns. First, Herodotus shows that the liberation of the Medes, "brave men," from Assyrian despotism, which had seemed a change from evil to good, leads in fact to anarchy. Second, Deioces does not use evil means to obtain an evil goal but gets the Medes to accept tyranny by the paradoxical device of acquiring a reputation as a just and good man.

We first meet the Medes almost in a state of nature, for, like noble savages, they live apart from other people "in separate villages," κατὰ κώμας, and by their own customs: "independently," αὐτόνομοι.⁷ But although free from their Assyrian lords and brave on the battlefield, the Medes experience lawlessness (ἀνομίης) and suffer injustice from one another, and so they look to Deioces. Although already respected in his own village, Deioces applies himself strenuously to the pursuit of "righteousness," δικαιοσύνην, because he knows, says Herodotus, that "justice is the enemy of injustice," τῷ δικαίῳ τὸ ἄδικον πολέμιον. The Medes, respecting Deioces' reputation, choose him as "judge," δικαστήν, and he, aiming at "kingship" (ἀρχήν), remains "honest and just" (ἰθύς τε καὶ δίκαιος ἦν [1.96.2]). Clearly Deioces values these qualities of honesty and fairness only as a means to his goal of rule over the Medes.

What had begun as an apparently cautionary tale about the career of an evil man or perhaps an illustration of the pusillanimity of the Medes turns into a folktale about the origins of monarchy. The highly abstract language and the absence of particularizing details in the story suggest not the history of a real individual but a symbolic tale of how the first king came into existence. Later, once Deioces is king and establishes rules for his court, Herodotus comments that "Deioces was the first to establish this procedure," κόσμον τόνδε Δηιόκης πρῶτός ἐστι ὁ καταστησάμενος (1.99.1).

Herodotus, continuing his story, emphasizes Deioces' judicial role in great detail. The multiple repetitions of words with the DIK root even suggest that Herodotus is punning on Deioces' (Δηιόκης) own name.⁸ Deioces wins praise because of his fair judgments (κατὰ τὸ ὀρθὸν δικάζων) and because of the unjust judgments (ἀδίκοισι γνώμῃσι) of others. The people are eager to receive judgment (δικασόμενοι) from him (1.96.3). When the reliability of Deioces' judgment (δίκας) becomes known, his popularity grows. Deioces now announces he will no longer sit in judgment (ἐδίκαζε) and refuses to judge (δικᾶν) any more, saying that he gets no profit from his judging (δικάζειν) all day long (1.97.1).

Because Deioces no longer shares his wisdom, lawlessness breaks out even more virulently than before and turns to "violence," ἁρπαγῆς (1.97.2). Deioces' plan is now clear: he will make the Medes want him to continue to maintain justice and good judgments, and so they will, apparently on their own; but actually because of Deioces' plan, they ask him to become their king. This passage heightens the reader's sense of the paradox of Deioces' actions. The repetition of words meaning "justice" and "judgment" remind us of how a reputation for scrupulous fairness will help Deioces achieve tyranny. His plea that he does not profit from his career as a just man contrasts his apparent selflessness with his underlying selfish motives.

Herodotus continues to delay the conclusion of the story not merely to prolong the reader's anticipation but to add more significant details. Herodotus describes how the Medes reach their decision: first, they discuss their problem; second, they decide they need a king; third, they debate who the king should be; finally, they decide to ask Deioces to rule them (1.97.2–98.1). In this passage we hear for the first time, in an apparently cynical aside, of "friends" (φίλοι) of Deioces who, while Deioces stays aloof from the debate, represent his interests. The existence of such a cadre reveals that the clever Deioces had planned far in advance for such a moment and that his chief interest is not to prove to his fellow Medes the advantages of central authority or to ensure good government for the Medes, but to gain and wield power himself.

Deioces refuses to accept kingship, however, unless he also gets all the external symbols and signs of royalty. Deioces specifies that the Medes must build a series of fortified palaces that will be "worthy of his office" (ἄξια τῆς βασιληίης) and give him a personal bodyguard of spear bearers (δορυφόροισι). The Medes must also leave their village life to reside in a new city capital, Agbatana, girded by seven concentric walls. "The outermost of these walls," says Herodotus, "is about the size of the walls of Athens" (1.98.2–6). The common people of the Medes (τὸν δὲ ἄλλον δῆμον) live outside these walls, whereas Deioces secludes himself within the innermost ring from any contact with his subjects, concludes all business through messengers (δι' ἀγγέλων), and forbids laughing and spitting in his presence. Deioces isolates himself even from his boyhood friends (ὁμήλικες) so that none of them can reflect that they are just as good as he and plot against him. Herodotus records Deioces' thought that "if none of his subjects saw him, they would consider him different [ἑτεροῖος, i.e., superior] from themselves" (1.99).

In this catalogue of the trappings of tyranny, every detail conjures up for an Athenian audience the typical tyrant of tragedy, whose power rests on the threat of force, who exercises power secretly and apart from the people he rules and whose revolution he fears and expects. An apparently offhand but calculated comparison of the walls of Agbatana and Athens and characterization of the Medes as a δῆμος naturally leads the reader to contrast oriental tyranny and Hellenic democracy. Greeks live inside, not outside the walls of their cities and shun egregious display of wealth in their private dwellings. Deioces styles himself superior in every way to his fellow men (although he admits privately this is not true), whereas all the Greeks who are ἄνδρες ἀγαθοί (Herodotus' description of the Medes) acknowledge one another as equals. To be followed by an armed guard—in fact, to be armed in any way within a city—is repugnant to the Greeks because it suggests a rule by violence.[9]

Deioces' elaborate safeguards proportionately increase the reader's suspicion that once in power Deioces' true character will reveal itself and he will turn into a savage and ruthless ruler. Indeed, Herodotus seems to be building to a dramatic and climactic reversal: the revelation of Deioces' true character to the Medes, whose position will be a pitiable one of having been duped and betrayed, of having won their freedom from their Assyrian rulers only to become enslaved again. But none of this happens, for, in a surprise twist to what the storyteller has led his audience to expect, Deioces remains as just and as wise as before he became ruler: "Now that he had made himself secure in his tyranny [ἐκράτυνε ἑωυτὸν τῇ τυραννίδι], he was strict in his stewardship of justice," τὸ δίκαιον (1.100.1). Deioces has his subjects submit their judicial complaints to him in writing and punishes any he finds guilty of outrageous acts (ὑβρίζοντα). Deioces also appoints "spies" (κατάσκοποι) to aid him in ferreting out wrongdoers (1.100.2).

Deioces remains remote from his subjects but only to decide their cases more impartially behind closed doors than would be possible face to face. His devotion to justice turns out to be genuine and disinterested after all. The ominous trappings and ceremonies actually help him to rule more wisely, for the palaces, guards, secret police, royal etiquette, and seclusion serve his subjects' interests by helping him to maintain absolute impartiality. Herodotus here contrives to show that the most obnoxious trappings of the tyrant—his remoteness from the people, his network of spies and enforcers, and his ability to punish according to whim and without fear of retribution—are all essential to the ideal monarchical state. Although Deioces deceives his subjects into thinking that he is superior to other men, he perpetuates this ruse for the Medes' ultimate benefit. Absolute power over the Medes does not seduce Deioces into expanding his power, for he remains satisfied with the throne of his own country alone (μοῦνον). The story highlights the contrast between the ideal rule of one truly good man, whose rule resembles that of the Platonic philosopher king and the stereotypic tyrant of tragedy. These, Herodotus believes, are the two extremes of good and evil possible in a monarchy. Simultaneously Herodotus emphasizes both the attractions and the dangers of autonomy. The blessings of independence quickly fade for the Medes as their freedom—before the intervention of Deioces—turns to lawlessness.

The story of Deioces has significant links with Herodotus' account of Pisistratus, another story that reveals the writer's sympathy with one-man rule. Just as Deioces begins his rise to power through a good reputation, πρότερον δόκιμος (1.96.2), so Pisistratus "had earlier won renown," πρότερον εὐδοκιμήσας (1.59.4), in a battle with Megara. Deioces gets the Medes to give him "spear bearers," δορυφόρους (1.98.2), and Pisistratus tricks the Athenians into giving him a bodyguard of whom Herodotus says, "They were not Pisistratus' spear bearers but his club bearers," δορυφόροι μὲν οὐκ ἐγένοντο Πεισιστράτου, κορυνηφόροι δέ (1.59.5). Deioces contrives to make the Medes offer him the rule. Pisistratus similarly tricks the Athenians into believing he has been drafted by Athena herself. Pisistratus dresses up a tall, handsome girl as Athena and has her drawn around the countryside in a wagon while heralds proclaim: "Athenians, receive Pisistratus with kindness, for Athena herself honors him above all men and leads him to her acropolis" (1.60.5). This bogus Athena and the heralds play the same part as the friends of Deioces who suggest one-man rule and the name of Deioces to the Medes (1.97.2–3). Herodotus may pun on the name of Deioces (=δίκη), but he certainly puns on the name of the tall girl who impersonates Athena: Φύη (=φυή, "stature") (1.60.4).[10] Deioces succeeds on his first try in becoming king of the Medes, but Pisistratus makes three attempts before finally securing power. Each time, however, he does manage to fool the credulous Athenians. Thus Herodotus demonstrates a point he makes elsewhere about the Athenians: "It is easier to deceive a multitude than one man" (5.97.2).[11]

Without Deioces, the Medes suffer from ἀνομίη, "lawlessness." Without Pisistratus—or before his rule becomes firmly established—the Athenians suffer from στάσις, "factionalism," a word that occurs seven times in the passage. When Croesus inquires into the condition of the Athenians, whom the Pythia recommends to him as allies, he learns they are διεσπασμένον, "torn by factionalism," but κατεχόμενον, "held in check," by Pisistratus (1.59.1). Previously, Athens had been persistently troubled by feuds among partisans of Chilon, Megacles, and Pisistratus himself, but Pisistratus' accession to one-man rule ends this instability. Finally, just as Deioces surprises the reader by the steadfastness of his justice even after he has absolute power, so Pisistratus reveals his underlying good will toward Athens once he has, with the aid of his club bearers, taken the Acropolis: "Then Pisistratus ruled Athens, not disturbing the existing offices and not changing the laws, but he managed the city according to those then in effect and arranged all fairly and well," . . . οὔτε τιμὰς τὰς ἐούσας συνταράξας οὔτε θέσμια μεταλλάξας, ἐπί τε τοῖσι κατεστεῶσι ἔνεμε τὴν πόλιν κοσμέων καλῶς τε καὶ εὖ (1.59.6).[12]

Herodotus' clearest enunciation of the idea that one-man rule is best—so long as that one man is perfectly good and wise—occurs in the speech of Darius in the Conspirators' Debate (3.82). In fact, all three of the speeches in this debate as well as the circumstances in which the debate occurs shed light on the motif of the philosopher king and suggest parallels among the accession stories of Deioces, Pisistratus, and Darius. Like Deioces and Pisistratus, Darius deviously plots to secure one-man rule, and though Darius does not succeed as a ruler as well as they, he too tries to rule well.

The accession of Darius, like the accessions of Deioces and Pisistratus, ends a period of unstable or irregular rule. After the death of Cambyses an impostor priest, the pseudo-Smerdis, rules Persia. A group of six Persian nobles, led by Otanes, discovers the fraud (3.69). They gather at Susa where, happening to meet Darius, they share their knowledge of the deception with him: "Since he had come the six decided to make him an ally. The group, now seven, gathered to deliberate [ἐδίδοσαν σφίσι λόγους] and exchange pledges" (3.71.1). After the rest have shared with Darius their discovery of the treachery of the pseudo-Smerdis and their plans for assassinating the pretender, Darius suddenly announces that he knew about the real identity of the pseudo-Smerdis all along: "When it came to Darius to speak, he said, 'I thought that I alone knew that the Magus was ruling and that Smerdis, the son of Cyrus, had died. It was for this reason that I have come in haste in order to plan the death of the Magus'" (3.71.2).

Darius' words are hardly convincing. He is the first to mention that he has come to Susa "in haste." Herodotus introduced his arrival by simply saying, "he arrived," παραγίγνεται, and with no suggestion of a planned mission. Darius, in fact, as he quietly listens and waits his turn to speak, is using this time to make quick plans. He may have had ambitions before, but now when he hears that the Smerdis ruling Persia is a fraud—which he pretends to have known before—he takes action not only to kill the Magus but to become king.[13] The political situation in Persia now exactly resembles that in Media before the accession of Deioces: there is disorder that results in a debate about a possible course of action (ἐδίδοσαν σφισι λόγον, λέγοντες περὶ τῶν κατηκόντων [1.97.2]). But before the Persians can turn to the question of what system of government will be best for them, there is a discussion of how to eliminate the impostor. In this discussion Darius seizes the leadership of

the group from Otanes, who counsels delay (3.71.3), suggests
their group needs more recruits (3.71.3), and worries about
how to overcome the palace guards (3.72.1). Darius responds
to Otanes' equivocation: "Otanes, there are many things which
are hard to make clear in speech [λόγῳ μέν], but not in action
[ἔργῳ δέ] and also things explicable in words [λόγῳ μέν], but in
fact [ἔργῳ δέ] no splendid deed proceeds from them" (3.72.2).

In outlining the strategy by which he proposes to gain
access to the palace, Darius says he will claim that his father
Hystaspes has sent him with a message for Smerdis. Darius then
tries, through a lengthy digression, to justify telling this falsehood:

> A lie must be told, but let it be so. Men strive for the same goal
> whether they lie or tell the truth. They tell lies when they expect
> to gain from persuading others of their falsehoods and tell the
> truth when they hope benefit will accrue to them and their
> listeners will hearken to them. Though they act differently they
> arrive at the same goal. If there were no hope of gain the honest
> man and the liar would be the same. (3.72)

Darius will tell a lie to gain access to the palace. Earlier he lied
to his fellow conspirators when he claimed he came "in haste in
order to plan the death of the Magus" (3.71.2, cf. 70.1). But his
speech speaks explicitly only to the lie he will use to perpetrate
the plot against the pseudo-Smerdis. Of his lie to them, the
conspirators are unaware. Darius' argument that the ends justify the means excuses his own hidden plans to himself. This
argument also explains the morality of Deioces and Pisistratus.
Each tricks his subjects but does so only to attain some gain or
higher good.

Once the conspirators succeed—with Darius himself
striking the fatal blow—in murdering the pseudo-Smerdis, they
debate the new system of government. Again, as before the
accession of Deioces, this debate is an expanded version of the
discussion that took place in Media. The Medes had to choose
between anarchy and monarchy, but in the speeches of Otanes,
Megabyzus, and Darius, Herodotus gives the Persians three
choices: democracy, oligarchy, or monarchy.

Otanes' speech in favor of democracy (ἰσονομίη) comes first, but his arguments are vague and, in comparison with the speeches that follow, brief. Otanes argues in generalities such as "democracy has the fairest of all names" (3.80.6). Only a third of his speech in fact bears on the form of government he champions. Because he apparently cannot think of positive arguments for democracy, Otanes concentrates instead on the evils of one-man rule. But the examples of kings in Herodotus do not strongly support his criticisms and, in the cases of Pisistratus and Deioces, even offer significant exceptions to them. Otanes uses Cambyses and the pseudo-Smerdis as his examples of bad monarchs, but they are not convincing choices since Cambyses was deranged (3.33) and the pseudo-Smerdis, an impostor, might be said not to be a real king at all. Otanes' speech, therefore, is weak and unconvincing because he does not advance specific arguments for democracy and because his case against monarchy is contradicted by important passages in the *Histories*.[14]

Otanes also argues that even a good man, once king, will be corrupted by the power he wields: "Suppose you set up [as king] the best of all men, he will soon abandon his former ways of thinking." Otanes thinks a king by nature acts outrageously (ἐγγίνεται μὲν γὰρ οἱ ὕβρις) because of his power and will remain jealous of others despite all that he possesses himself (3.80.3). He will be open to informers and gossip, crave flattery, and be hard to please. All these are stereotypic attributes of the tyrannical personality. Yet both Deioces and Pisistratus avoid these vices to remain uncorrupted by the power they possess.

Otanes' "most important points" (3.80.5) come at the conclusion of his denunciation of monarchy: a monarch changes ancestral laws (νόμαιά τε κινέει πάτρια), rapes women, and puts people to death without trial. Of these crimes the first is the least convincing as a universal trait of tyrants, since Herodotus has specifically mentioned that Pisistratus governed, "not disturbing the existing offices nor changing the laws" (1.59.6). Furthermore, Darius, in his speech in favor of one-man rule, argues for monarchy because it is a traditional form of Persian government: "My opinion . . . is that we ought not to destroy

our ancestral customs [πατρίους νόμους] since they are good
and there are none better" (3.82.5). And though Deioces forces
the Medes to abandon their custom of living in separate villages, his regime does represent a return for them to totalitarian
rule: αὖτις ἐς τυραννίδας περιῆλθον (1.96.1). In arguing that
democracy will be good for Persia, Otanes contradicts himself,
for he proposes to change the traditional form of government.
This violation of ancient custom is just the practice of which he
accuses tyrants. Otanes also brings up the more serious charges
of rape and murder, but tyrants hardly have a monopoly on
these crimes, and certainly Deioces and Pisistratus avoid them.

The next speaker, Megabyzus, agrees with Otanes
about monarchy but champions oligarchy. Yet he too, like
Otanes, does not muster evidence for his case but instead attacks
democracy. Whereas Otanes criticizes monarchy for faults that
Herodotus shows kings do not or need not possess, Herodotus
proves valid the arguments Megabyzus uses against democracy.
Megabyzus' speech thus makes clear that in his defense of democracy Otanes does not speak for Herodotus. Otanes' speech
comes first not because Herodotus believes Otanes' arguments
are right but so that the cumulative arguments of Megabyzus and
Darius can prove them wrong: democracy is not the best but the
worst of the three systems.[15] Megabyzus argues: "Nothing is
more witless nor more prone to outrageous acts than the useless
mob," ὁμίλου γὰρ ἀχρηίου οὐδέν ἐστι ἀξυνετώτερον οὐδὲ
ὑβριστότερον (3.81.1). The stories of Deioces and Pisistratus
prove this point. The Medes are incapable of ruling themselves,
and who would entrust the rule to men willing to believe that a
tall girl in armor is Athena?[16]

Megabyzus, who excoriates the chaotic way a mob
thinks and acts and compares its behavior to a river in torrent,
concedes to Darius in advance a point against Otanes' condem-
nation of tyranny by acknowledging that, in comparison with
the mob, a tyrant is "rational," γιγνώσκων (3.81.2). Megabyzus, however, closes his speech with the disingenuously self-
congratulatory statement that the new oligarchy of the best will
be composed of "men such as we ourselves are" (3.81.3), and
he anticipates Darius' far more modest and convincing appeal to
his own preeminent role in deposing the Magus.

Darius' speech imperviously resists criticism by stressing the absolutely ideal case of the tyranny of a perfectly good and wise man: "Nothing could be better than the finest man, for with the finest intelligence he can manage the affairs of the multitude in a manner beyond reproach" (3.82.2). Yet Darius also acknowledges the necessity for secrecy and, by implication, deceit in government, for this has been his own approach. Indeed, he alludes to his earlier arguments in favor of attacking the Magus instantly before the plot can be betrayed: "He [the monarch] is best able to keep his plans quiet and away from the ears of malicious men" (3.82.2).

Although he speaks at no greater length than his predecessors in the debate, Darius manages to say more about monarchy than Otanes and Megabyzus do about democracy or oligarchy because he avoids detailed criticisms of other forms of government. Darius points out the failures of oligarchy but only in order to show how monarchy will solve them. Ultimately, Darius argues, the breakdown of oligarchy will lead the people to recognize the advantages of monarchy: "In oligarchy strong hostilities inevitably emerge among the many who vie to serve the state. Because each man thinks of himself as a leader and thinks that his ideas are best, all come to be hostile to one another. From these hostilities come political factions [στάσεις] and from these factions [στασίων] comes bloodshed, and because of bloodshed the state resorts to monarchy" (3.82.3). The breakdown of democracy into anarchy similarly illustrates the need for discipline imposed by a strong central authority:

When the people [δῆμος] rules, mischief is inevitable, and when there is mischief in public affairs, the basest elements resolve their differences and form strong associations instead. These seek to undermine the public good, and this continues until someone of the people comes forward to put a stop to it. For this reason he becomes the object of people's admiration and this admiration leads to his appearance as sole ruler. (3.82.4)

Just as Darius' remarks about the emergence of monarchy from oligarchy through "factions" recall the experience of Pisistratus, so his statement that the bloodshed of democracy leads also to monarchy recalls Deioces, who indeed becomes king precisely because he is "the object of the people's admiration."

Darius' arguments in favor of monarchy win because they are convincing to the other conspirators (except for Otanes and Megabyzus). The purpose of the debate is to present a true discussion on the merits of three systems of rule and not to state an obvious point, namely, Darius did become king, and arguments in favor of monarchy (if there was a question of a change) must have prevailed. The debate is a real contest. Monarchy wins. Not only the speeches and their context but similarities with the stories of Deioces and Pisistratus show that the Conspirators' Debate forms part of a pattern. The debate is part of the story of Darius, which also illustrates the positive possibilities of one-man rule through the motif of the philosopher king.

Once Darius wins the debate, however, the question of who is to fill the role of the ideal king Darius has described remains open, just as after the partisans of Deioces convince the Medes that they need a king, there must be further debate before the choice actually falls on Deioces. But after the debate in Persia there is action, not more words. The conspirators agree to ride out at daybreak and crown as their king the man whose horse first neighs at the sunrise (3.84.3). Earlier in his speech in favor of monarchy, Darius argued that the Persians had succeeded in freeing themselves from the Magus because of "one man" and so should in the future be ruled by one man, but he modestly did not mention his own name. Yet it was Darius' plan and Darius' hand that killed the impostor. Darius obviously believes he should be king of Persia and, like Deioces, contrives a scheme to make his selection inevitable. Darius' groom cleverly prompts his master's stallion to perform at the proper moment (3.85). The ruse is amusing and undignified (like that which secured Pisistratus' return from exile), but Herodotus ennobles the moment by having a peal of thunder confirm the conspirators' choice.[17]

Finally, like Deioces and Pisistratus, Darius plots deviously to gain this throne, but once in power he rules as well and as honestly as he can. His first official acts as king (after setting up a statue to commemorate the groom's help) are to divide the country into easily governable satrapies and to arrange for the orderly payment of taxes. Because the manner of Darius' accession so closely resembles those of Deioces and Pisistratus, he has the potential, in Herodotus' view, to become a truly wise and perfect king. Darius clearly knows what constitutes a good monarchy since he has just eloquently articulated the principles of an ideal monarchy in the Conspirators' Debate.

As a whole, however, the actual career of Darius falls far short of the high standards set by Deioces and by Darius' speech. He fails to put into practice what he had so cogently explained in theory and thus proves his own statement that some things are "clear in principle" (λόγῳ μέν) but often lead to "no actual notable result" (ἔργον οὐδέν . . . λαμπρόν). Darius behaves with senseless cruelty, for example, and is manipulated by his far more clever wife, Atossa. The two most important respects, however, in which Darius fails to live up to Deioces' standards are in intelligence and discipline. Because he is extraordinarily intelligent Deioces never needs to seek advice and thus share his power, and, of course, he never makes a mistake. But Darius not only seeks but misuses advice, for he rejects such wise counsel as that of Coes (4.97) and yet succumbs to the deceitful proposals of Histiaeus (5.107). Deioces' rule is truly a monarchy, the rule of an individual, but Darius, by turning to others, both admits his fallibility and ultimately transforms his kingship into a system of government that is closer to oligarchy. Yet Darius, although he is able to see that the accessibility of his predecessor makes him vulnerable and so can formulate a plan to kill the pseudo-Smerdis and carry it out, fails, once king himself, to apply this knowledge and experience to his own position. Darius behaves negligently when he does not seclude himself from the other six conspirators, and this proves to be the cause of mischief for him. Deioces, we recall, totally isolated himself from his boyhood friends so that they would not reflect that he is no better than they and plot against him. In fact, Deioces conducts all his business "through messengers," δι' ἀγγέλων (1.99.1).

Darius' speech also warns against the dangers of oligarchs plotting against one another (3.82.3). But Darius acquiesces in an ultimately dangerous arrangement, for he agrees that once he is king of Persia any of the conspirators may approach him "without being announced" (ἄνευ ἐσαγγελέος) except when he is sleeping with a woman (3.84.2). This last proviso shows that the six conspirators will have almost total access to the king, for he is only unavailable during the most intimate moments. This easy access to the king could facilitate exactly the kind of attack by which the conspirators removed the pseudo-Smerdis from power, a king who obviously failed to guard himself sufficiently. Darius' comment about the proposed attack against the pseudo-Smerdis—"Because we are men of rank, none will oppose us, whether out of respect or fear" (3.72.3)—reveals exactly the potential danger Darius faces from his former fellow conspirators.

An incident that occurs just after Darius has become king illustrates Darius' laxness (3.118–119). Intaphernes, wanting to conduct business with Darius, is told by the doorkeeper and the usher that he may not enter because, as is actually the case, the king is having intercourse. But Intaphernes thinks they are lying and assaults and hideously mutilates the two servants before leaving. When Darius sees the savage attack on his servants, he instantly takes fright that the other five conspirators have joined with Intaphernes to overthrow him. Yet he could have foreseen these circumstances from Megabyzus' critique of oligarchy and his own experiences with the Magus. He interrogates the five and, learning that they are not party to a coup attempt, confines his dreadful punishment, death for the (falsely) accused conspirator and all his posterity, to Intaphernes. Darius here fulfills Otanes' predictions about the monarch's fear and cruelty instead of his own about the king's wisdom and justice. Herodotus' judgment is clear. Like Periander on the advice of Thrasyboulus (5.92ζ), Darius should have "cut down the tallest sheaves of wheat" in his body politic. He should have eliminated his fellow conspirators and any Persians prominent enough to pose a threat to his rule early in his reign, and he should have copied Deioces by closing off public access to the king absolutely.[18]

Remarkable similarities between the Conspirators' Debate and a hitherto neglected passage in Book Two provide independent confirmation that Herodotus' sympathies in the debate—as well as in the stories of Deioces and Pisistratus—lie with the idea of one-man rule. Psammetichus comes to be pharaoh after a period in Egyptian history during which the country experiments with democratic and then oligarchic rule before reverting to monarchy (2.147–152). Scholars have paid little attention to this passage except to note that the events recorded are not confirmed by any documents from Egypt, a fact suggesting that Herodotus may be creating or freely adapting from some sophistic source a story that illustrates his own ideas.[19] He describes how after the unpopular rule of a priest of Hephaestus, the Egyptians "become free," ἐλευθερωθέντες, but shortly afterward find themselves unable to "manage," διαιτᾶσθαι, without a king. The Egyptians establish twelve kings, who together rule a country divided into twelve "portions," μοίρας (2.147). But then a dispute arises, which leads to the accession of Psammetichus, one of the twelve, as sole ruler (2.151–152). The Conspirators' Debate, held in the aftermath of the impostor priest, promises Persia a similar sequence of democracy, oligarchy, and one-man rule. These events in Egypt, moreover, illustrate the truth of Megabyzus' arguments against democracy in the Conspirators' Debate (that the *demos* cannot govern itself [3.81]) and of Darius' arguments against oligarchy (that the quarrels of oligarchs will result in monarchy [3.82]). In addition, both Darius and Psammetichus begin their reigns by commemorating, through dedications, the fortuity that led them to their thrones (3.88; 2.153) and by implementing elaborate and successful schemes of imperial organization (3.89–95; 2.153).

Although we never learn enough about Psammetichus and his later career to be able to assign to him definitely the role of philosopher king, the story of his accession sheds great light on Darius' arguments against oligarchy and follows closely—but in telescoped form—the pattern of events in Persia at the time of the Conspirators' Debate. We do not know if Sethus, the priest who ruled Egypt before Psammetichus, was an impostor like the pseudo-Smerdis, but he was a priest and

Herodotus does tell us that his rule was irregular and unpopular (2.141). We never learn how Sethus was removed, but some coup or assassination may be inferred, similar to the story of Darius. Herodotus also gives no details of why the Egyptians were unable to "manage" without a king, but the story of Deioces supplies a plausible scenario of lawlessness and violence. We also do not know how the twelve oligarchs of Egypt come to be in power, but they clearly play a role similar to the seven conspirators in Persia. In Egypt, however, the twelve follow the advice of Megabyzus rather than that of Darius by governing the country themselves as an oligarchy rather than choosing one man as sole ruler. Herodotus describes the terms, presumably the result of discussion among them, under which the twelve agree to rule Egypt: "not to attack one another, not to seek to have more than any other has, and to be firm friends" (2.147.3). Intermarriage, the same bond sought by the seven Persian conspirators (3.84.2), secures their pact. A peculiar circumstance also draws the twelve Egyptian rulers together and makes their cooperation essential to this political arrangement. There is a prophecy that "he who first pours a libation from a bronze vessel in the temple of Hephaestus will rule all of Egypt" (2.147.4). The twelve oligarchs have agreed to prevent the prophecy's fulfillment, so clearly they rule *together* an Egypt divided into twelve provinces rather than as independent tyrants.[20]

The prophecy is fulfilled during a meeting of the twelve rulers at the temple of Hephaestus, an assembly that confirms the cooperative nature of their rule. At this fateful meeting, however, the priest handing out golden cups for the libation has none, as it happens, for Psammetichus, who, without thinking, uses his bronze helmet instead and thus fulfills the prophecy. Chance thus plays a role in the selection of Psammetichus as well as of Darius. The chance neighing of a horse proclaims Darius king, a chance drink from his bronze helmet makes Psammetichus king, though no cynical manipulation of fate takes place in the latter case. What happens next to Psammetichus recalls Darius' treatment of Intaphernes, although the situation is reversed, for it is the oligarchs who abuse Psammetichus, whom they suspect of having aimed at the monarchy, rather than the monarch maltreating the man suspected of leading an oligarchic coup. But in either case, the point of the story is the same: oligarchy—even a monarchy that shares some features of an oligarchy—is a treacherous political system. The other eleven oligarchs, believing Psammetichus acted by design, torture him. Upon discovering that he poured the offering by accident, they agree not to kill him but to strip him of his power and banish him to the swamps of Egypt.

But Psammetichus eventually manages to lead a rebellion, return from exile, defeat the eleven oligarchs, and establish himself as the sole ruler of Egypt. Psammetichus' first act after becoming king is to give handsome presents to the temple of Hephaestus at which he luckily carried out the prophecy (2.153). This act links Psammetichus to Darius, who also begins his reign by commemorating the good luck that brought him the crown when he sets up a statue of his groom. The story of Psammetichus' accession thus justifies the rule of kings in Egypt just as the Conspirators' Debate justifies the rule of kings in Persia. The Egyptians fail to rule themselves, and because the oligarchs cannot cooperate successfully, their rule, as Darius says it must, leads to monarchy.

The stories of Deioces, Pisistratus, Darius, and Psammetichus illustrate the idea that one-man rule by a good man will result in good government. But what if the ruler is less than perfect or even evil? If the superiority of one-man rule rests wholly on a man's moral character, it is a tenuous superiority. Darius' failures, for example, show that the best intentions may not have the best result. In the career of the Egyptian pharaoh Amasis, however, Herodotus explores a case where even a bad man proves to be an efficient and competent ruler. If Deioces is the best of men, Amasis is the worst, and the two stories, as Herodotus writes them, are mirror images of one another. Many links between the story of Amasis and those of other philosopher kings show that Herodotus is here demonstrating that under certain conditions monarchy, even if the king is a scoundrel, may still be the best system of government.

A portentous but accidental event also involving a bronze helmet brings Amasis, like Psammetichus, to the throne. We first meet Amasis when, just an ordinary soldier, he is sent by the pharaoh Apries to quell a rebellion in the kingdom. Amasis addresses the rebels, and, as he speaks, someone "stood behind Amasis and put a helmet on his head, saying that he was crowning 'the king'" (2.162.1). Amasis is "not unwilling," οὔ κως ἀεκού-σιον, and so, without delay, the rebels "set him up as king" (2.162.2). Later, Amasis admits: "I have for some time been planning to do this" (2.162.4). As in the case of Darius, a chance event—his "crowning" by one of the rebels—gives Amasis a sudden idea to act on his own ambitions.

Amasis fits the type of the philosopher king because once sole ruler, even though he has obtained his throne illegally, he rules well. He acts mildly toward the deposed Apries, whom he puts to death only reluctantly at the insistence of the Egyptian people (2.169). He shows his intelligence by dividing his days between work and relaxation, a way of life he justifies in a wise and witty speech: "You string a bow when it is needed and unstring it when it is not. If you kept it strung all the time it might break and you would not be able to use it when you needed to. Such is man's nature. If you take yourself seriously always and give no share of time to amusements, before you know it you will either become crazy or apoplectic" (2.173.3–4). Alone of Herodotus' ruling monarchs, Amasis acts the part of a wise adviser. The advice he gives to Polycrates about curtailing ambition contains the same tragic perception of life as we hear from Croesus: "Your great good fortune does not give me pleasure because I know that god is jealous" (3.40.2).[21] But Amasis does not, like Croesus, have to suffer defeat and lose his throne to acquire wisdom. Most important, Herodotus concludes that nothing "untoward," ἀνάρσιον, ever happened to Egypt during Amasis' rule (3.10.2) and that during his reign Egypt "prospered as never before," μάλιστα δὴ τότε εὐδαιμονῆσαι (2.177).

With his wise advice to Polycrates and good sense about his own life, Amasis most closely resembles Deioces among the philosopher kings in his intelligence. But in other respects Amasis is the extreme opposite of Deioces. Deioces, though he begins as a simple shepherd, assiduously cultivates conventional aristocratic pomp, not allowing either laughing or spitting in his presence (1.99). Amasis, too, is a "commoner," δημότην, and even among these "of obscure family," οἰκίης οὐκ ἐπιφανέος (2.172); but Amasis makes no attempt to put on airs or conceal his background, and his first public act on the stage of history is to break wind. When Apries urges Amasis to give up his revolt, Amasis confronts the messenger: "He rose in the saddle, for he happened to be on horseback, farted [ἀπεματάϊσε] and told him to take *this* [τοῦτο] back to Apries" (2.162.3). Amasis' crude gesture marks him as a blunt, straightforward type and a man with a sense of humor. Once established as pharaoh, Amasis' personal regimen proves eccentric. For half of every day he attends to affairs of state "with a will," but the rest of the day he spends relaxing: "He drank and told jokes with his boon companions and was silly and sportive" (2.173.1). Even his friends complain that he does not show sufficient respect for "the dignity of his throne," θρόνῳ σεμνῷ (2.173.2). How different was the behavior of Deioces, who demanded palaces "worthy of his sovereignty," ἄξια τῆς βασιληίης (1.98.2).

Amasis neither isolates nor elevates himself by means of guards or ceremonials but remains a man of the people who continues to pursue the friendship of his old friends. Amasis, in fact, uses a blasphemous practical joke to convince his subjects that *even though he is no better than they,* he deserves to rule. Amasis takes a gold slop basin used for washing banqueters' feet, has it made into an image of a god, and sets it up in a temple for the Egyptians to worship. Amasis next summons the Egyptians and points out to them that they are paying honor to an object that was formerly a vessel in which they had "vomited, urinated, and washed their feet." Therefore, argues Amasis, the Egyptians ought to honor him despite his earlier humble station in life. "By this means," says Herodotus, "he convinced the Egyptians to serve him" (2.172.3–5). In other words, Amasis directly confronts the Egyptians with his commonness and does so, in a characteristic way, by a crude joke. His behavior differs radically from that of Deioces, for he does not ignore his humble origins but calls attention to them, whereas Deioces, once in power, attempts to create an aura around himself to set him apart and make his subjects believe that he is "different from them," ἑτεροῖος (1.99.2). Herodotus comments that Amasis achieves his aims "by cleverness . . . not by arrogance," σοφίη . . . οὐκ ἀγνωμοσύνη (2.172.2).

Before Amasis became king, he had lived, we learn, the life of a profligate and a scoundrel: "He was a drunkard and a prankster and not at all a serious person" (2.174.1). Amasis had actually turned to thievery. Whenever he was caught, he submitted to the arbitration of various oracles, and although sometimes denounced by the god he was on other occasions exonerated. When he becomes king, Amasis neglects and makes no offering at the oracles that had earlier exonerated him as an honest man but favors only those that had correctly called him a thief (2.174.2). Here Amasis publicly acknowledges his life of crime—he is the antithesis of the upright Deioces—but also demonstrates his justness, a characteristic in which, as a philosopher king, he closely resembles Deioces.[22]

Amasis' career illustrates the truth of Darius' statement that "some things are hard to explain in words, but not in action" (3.72.2), for in theory a rogue like Amasis should become an evil tyrant, but in fact Amasis is a remarkably good ruler. The career of Amasis offers the reader the same kind of surprise as that of Deioces. Neither king commits the outrages that an earlier pattern of behavior promised. Power does not, even in the case of Amasis, corrupt a bad man. In fact, Amasis' career demonstrates the falsity of Otanes' claim that power inevitably corrupts kings. Amasis manages to live in private the raffish life he prefers, but in public he rules with honesty and intelligence.[23]

Deioces is remote and omniscient whereas Pisistratus, a clever trickster, anticipates Themistocles. Darius, in turn, foreshadows Xerxes, for both are good men and well meaning but weak, erratic, and unable to use effectively their occasional real insights. Most interesting and unusual is Amasis, a hedonist and a scoundrel, but a man able to turn his energies disinterestedly to the service of the state. Herodotus uses these stories to show that the superiority of monarchy as a system of rule does not depend absolutely on the character of the man who rules.

When Herodotus advocates one-man rule over democracy, he is only agreeing with the main current of Greek opinion. Democracy was deplored in antiquity as a bad form of government and treated only as a necessary evil. The funeral oration that Thucydides places in the mouth of Pericles (2.35–46) stands in splendid isolation in the surviving literature of the fifth century B.C. But even this radiant speech Thucydides undercuts by the immediately succeeding description of the plague, in which Pericles himself died (2.47–54), and by the statement that Athens in the days of Pericles was a democracy in name only, since Pericles actually ruled alone (2.65.9). Later generations read the funeral oration with the ironic knowledge of hindsight that Athens lost the Peloponnesian war and her democracy never fulfilled the bright promise of its early Periclean years.

In this context and in view of Herodotus' evident sympathies for monarchy, his praises of freedom, though the passages are well known and often quoted, now take on new significance. Herodotus' positive feelings about political freedom do not, as is generally stated, stem from his experience of or esteem for Athenian democracy.[24] We might look, for example, at his comments on Athenian democracy after a reference to Athens' military success against the Chalcideans:

> Not in this one case alone but generally it is clear that an equal voice in state affairs [ἰσηγορίη] is a significant [σπουδαῖον] thing, since when the Athenians were governed by tyrants they were no better than their neighbors, but when they got rid of tyrants, they became by far the best. It seems that when they were held in check [κατεχόμενοι] they did not try their best because they were under the sway of a despot [δεσπότη], but when they were freed [ἐλευθερωθέντων], each one tried on his own to make the best possible effort. (5.78)

Herodotus feels he must explain in detail how democracy could result in military success, since this idea contradicts the theories current in his day; indeed, it runs counter to Demaratus' explanation for the success of the Spartans in battle because they obey νόμος as a δεσπότης. No doubt Herodotus does admire Athens but not blindly or without citing, as we have repeatedly seen, occasions when the Athenians behaved foolishly or weakly.

The origins of Herodotus' positive feelings lie, I think, rather in his celebration of the noble savage, who enjoys a form of freedom much more profound than political freedom. "When the Scythian kings heard of slavery," reports Herodotus, "they were enraged" (4.128). The Scythians and the Massagetae, for example, are not just free to speak their minds in public debate but free to live without sexual restrictions, without fields or harvests, and without cities (1.216; 4.46).

If freedom, for Herodotus, is one of the good things of life, it shares with life's other blessings certain dangers in addition to the inherent ones of anarchy and lack of discipline. In the *Histories,* as we can see in many passages in Greek literature, pleasure and happiness may be ominous conditions, for they may provoke divine jealousy and lead to disaster.[25] Herodotus writes: "God gives man a taste [γεύσας] of good fortune in his life and then ruins him utterly" (7.46). To this statement we may compare the Milesians' reluctance (6.5) "to accept another tyrant because they had tasted freedom" (οἷά τε ἐλευθερίης γευσάμενοι). Here and throughout the *Histories* Herodotus takes for granted that freedom is good, but not all men, therefore, ought to have freedom always, for too much freedom, just as too much prosperity, can provoke the jealousy of the gods. So in Herodotus just as some people are fated to suffer (through an inscrutable combination of divine envy and their own folly), some are destined not to enjoy and indeed appear not to deserve freedom.

The Samians offer a good example of a people who appear perfectly satisfied with tyranny and who would have been better off never to have experienced any other form of government. When Polycrates dies, next in line for the throne of Samos is a certain Maeandrius, who tries to introduce democracy (ἰσονομίη) in place of tyranny but fails disastrously.

Herodotus says of Maeandrius (3.142.1) that "though he wanted to be the justest of men [δικαιοτάτῳ], this was not to be [γενέσθαι οὐκ ἐξεγένετο]." Maeandrius inaugurates a change in the form of government by setting up an altar in a shrine dedicated to "Zeus the Freedom-Giver" ('Ελευθερίου), and then calling an "open meeting," ἐκκλησίην (3.142.2). At this meeting he announces that though he has the power to rule, he prefers not to "for I never liked the way Polycrates lorded it over other men who were just the same as he," δεσπόζων ἀνδρῶν ὁμοίων ἑωυτῳ (scruples, we may note, not shared by either Deioces or Amasis). Maeandrius now, in language reminiscent of Otanes' speech only a few pages earlier in the *Histories,* "proclaims" democracy: ἐς μέσον τὴν ἀρχὴν τιθεὶς ἰσονομίην ὑμῖν προαγορεύω (3.142.3). The only compensation Maeandrius asks for giving up his power is six talents from the property of Polycrates and the priesthood for himself and his family of the cult of Zeus the Freedom-Giver that he has just established.

The calamitous results of Maeandrius' apparently generous gesture of giving the Samians true freedom recall the arguments of Megabyzus against the evils of mob rule and those of Darius against oligarchy. A certain Telesarchus (a possible pun name) rises in the assembly after Maeandrius' announcement and denounces him as unfit to rule in any case because of low birth—though this was no hindrance to Amasis—and accuses him of embezzlement of state funds during the reign of Polycrates. Now, faced with a direct attack and the possibility that he will get nothing, neither the throne nor money and the priesthood, Maeandrius changes his mind, "realizing that if he gave up the throne another would be set up in his place" (3.143.1). He arrests the chief men of Samos (Thrasyboulus' advice again), but it is too late. Herodotus comments wryly at this point: "It appears that they [the Samians] did not want to be free" (3.143.2). Without a king and quarreling over a successor, the Samians are too disorganized to resist an attacking force of Persians led, ironically, by Otanes, the champion of democracy, who imposes the tyranny of the renegade Samian, Syloson. The story of Maeandrius and Samos shows that although political freedom may be good in theory, in practice many people are better off ruled by one man.[26]

The Ionians, too, do not deserve their freedom. These men, Herodotus says, are "blest with the fairest of climates" (1.142.1) and consequently are "the weakest of tribes" (1.143.2), or as the Scythians describe them: "the basest of free men and the best of slaves" (4.142). We often hear in the *Histories* the rallying cry: "Freedom for the Ionians!" but Herodotus shows that this is a meaningless phrase since the Ionians do not use their freedom well. Not only are they unable to govern themselves, but whenever freed, they soon fall again under Persian rule. When Bias suggests to the Ionians that they emigrate to Sardinia, where, he says, they will find both "freedom from slavery and great prosperity" (1.170), they ignore his advice. They do not possess sufficient self-discipline to tolerate military training let alone endure the rigors of combat (6.12), and not even the threat of enslavement moves them: "Men of Ionia, our affairs stand on a razor's edge. Will we be free men or slaves—and runaway slaves at that?" (6.11.2).

When Aristagoras lobbies at Sparta for aid against Persia for the Ionian revolt (5.49), his arguments are eloquent: "It is a great shame that the children of the Ionians should be slave instead of free." But Aristagoras has base, personal motives, which his speech reveals, for helping to free Ionia. The Spartans, as he shows, regardless of the Ionians, can get rich booty by attacking Persia. When the Athenians send a few ships to aid the revolt, Herodotus comments: "These ships were the beginning of many sorrows for both Greeks and barbarians" (5.97). Clearly the Athenians should have left the Ionians enslaved rather than provide the Persians with a pretext for the counterattack that led to the battle of Marathon. We can find corroboration for this interpretation of events when the Ionians "fall a third time under the Persians' yoke" (6.32). Herodotus shows that the Persians rule Ionia both mildly and fairly and that Artaphernes even forces the cities of the coast to make peace with one another (6.42).

Herodotus' treatment of freedom and tyranny as political alternatives in the individual state leads to the question of his views on the right of one state to subjugate another. But this is not an easy subject to discuss, for Herodotus does not distinguish clearly or consistently between national and international politics in his allusions to freedom and tyranny. We do not, however, find in the *Histories* the view, propounded by other Greek writers, that barbarians are born to be slaves and, conversely, Greeks to be free. Herodotus does show that some people at certain periods in their histories are incapable of ruling themselves and do not merit freedom. Greeks, for example the Samians and the Ionians, as well as barbarians fit this category. Herodotus believes it is better for the Ionians to be ruled by Persia than to wear themselves out in strife against one another, just as it is right for the boy Cyrus to rule his playmates because they have chosen him king (1.115). Herodotus shows that the rule of the aggressor is, in fact, beneficial to the Ionians, and he notes that the Persian tyranny even resulted in the establishment of democracies in some Greek cities by Mardonius. There may exist political circumstances to validate one nation's rule over another. When Herodotus reports that good government prevailed in some of these cases, we can see that he does not condemn such rule ipso facto. Yet Herodotus does condemn Xerxes for attempting to annex Greece. The natural boundaries between nations and empires, νομός in its meaning of "geographical region," provide the clue to Herodotus' thinking. He has a respect for νομοί that explains why he believes Xerxes may rule all of Asia but not any of Europe, or why Croesus may rule the coast of Asia Minor but ought not to cross to the islands.

Is it, in Herodotus' view, inevitable that there should be both rulers and ruled in the world? Just as in any body politic there will always be unruly citizens in need of the discipline of a strong government, in the world at large there will always be unruly nations like the Ionian cities, which, unable to regulate themselves, actually gain from their conquest by others. The ideal situation, however, if this were not true, would be for every nation to live apart from all others as do the Scythians and the Ethiopians, who not only keep within their national boundaries and apart from other people but do not even unite within their territories. Both prefer the loosest political and social organization—by tribes—to ensure themselves the greatest autonomy. Yet such independence, as Herodotus' portraits of these peoples show, depends on a simplicity of life and nobility of character that few nations possess.

For Herodotus it is one of the ironies of political life that most nations gain their own freedom only to enslave others. Here the Scythians and Ethiopians are anomalous. Although they are more powerful than their neighbors, they remain content within their own boundaries. With the possibility of easily subjugating neighboring tribes, they choose not to do so. But, as Herodotus repeatedly shows, for most nations one definition of freedom is, ironically, the right to enslave other peoples. The king who frees his people from another's domination also imposes his own. It is ironic that Persia, the prosperous aggressor, started out as a noble savage and that the Persians, intent on enslaving Greece, speak of themselves as liberated from the slavery of the Medes. Darius and his fellow conspirators call themselves "liberators," ἡμέας ἐλευθερωθέντας (3.82.5) even as they argue for a system of government in which all Persians will be slaves. Similarly, Hystaspes praises Cyrus for having "found the Persians slaves and made them free and *the rulers of others*" (1.210). In the *Histories* it is morally preferable for the powerful to resist the temptation to rule the weak even though the weak might profit from the arrangement.

It is often at the very moment that a people has gained its freedom that the idea comes to enslave another. So Themistocles triumphs over the Persian aggressor who had threatened to enslave him only to˙ attack the Andrians in an attempt to subjugate them (8.111–112). Similarly, Cyrus' counsel to the Persians, with which, significantly, Herodotus' book closes, contains this advice: the Persians may live in the plains and be slaves or live in the mountains and rule others (9.122.4). What is missing is a third alternative: for the Persians to remain in the mountains and keep to themselves. For this, Deioces is a model. Yet Herodotus sees this alternative as an anomaly that is possible only for a very few, like the exemplary Scythians and Ethiopians, and not a political reality. Herodotus, in this final remark, offers only a paradox: the blessings of freedom or discipline cannot be enjoyed, in either an open or a closed society, without suffering from their defects too. Herodotus presents the best case he finds for a closed society in the governments of Deioces and Amasis and for an open society in the noble lives of the Scythians and the Ethiopians, but he never forgets the darker side of this antithesis: brutal tyranny or mob rule.

CONCLUSION:
Anecdotes and History

Although early logographers, geographers, and compilers of lists as well as the epic and tragic poets influenced Herodotus' style, I have suggested in this study another essential ingredient not only for his style but for his thought: the nonliterary genre of the anecdote. In fact, I believe that anecdotes are not only the most characteristic aspect of Herodotus' style but also the most crucial for understanding how he composes his history and defines the genre. Before turning to my conclusions about the role of anecdotes in the *Histories,* I want first to deal with our attitude, whether conscious or unconscious, toward anecdotes, because our own biases about such stories can stand in the way of our appreciation of their role in the *Histories.*

The anecdote, although a form of narrative, differs from general narrative. Short, focused on a single, brief event, the anecdote reaches a definite conclusion and may center entirely on a climactic point. A general narrative concentrates on a sequence of events, often complexly related, and has a conclusion that is the result of prior events and not itself the purpose of the narrative, as often is the case with the characteristically pointed anecdote. Not only are anecdotes self-contained entities, they may have little or no link to any immediate context. These qualities of brevity, point, and lack of narrative context may quickly be transformed into pejorative terms. Anecdotes seem to readers at best a stylistic quirk, at worst a writer's weakness and a literary work's flaw. Their subject, perhaps amusing or even ribald, adds to the reader's bias against the seriousness of their writer. The "Secret History" ('Ανέκδοτα, unpublished works) of Procopius, a racy collection of the gossip of Justinian's court, has left its imprint on the somewhat discreditable meaning that anecdote usually implies for a reader.[1] If anecdotes represent a discreditable form of narrative, it is with a sense of irony that I assert their crucial role in the *Histories,* especially at a time when narrative itself, even the most rigorously factual, is under attack from some philosophers of history.[2] An anecdotal history then, as we may rightly characterize Herodotus' work, sounds like no history at all but a collection of amusing stories.

  But in Herodotus' day anecdotes had no such negative connotations, and in an oral culture their ephemeral nature did not count against them. This was an honorable genre, highly developed, we may presume, relative to the primitive crudeness of the first written prose works. It was these anecdotes, I maintain, that supplied the novel ingredient that makes the *Histories* its own unique literary genre. We cannot, however, directly study the anecdotes that inspired Herodotus, as we can study the influence of Homer, and trace Herodotus' borrowings and alterations. Comparative study of the motifs of world folklore, particularly as collected and identified by type in the monumental index of Stith Thompson, offers one useful style of analysis. We cannot doubt the existence in Herodotus' day of many short prose tales of the types now collected by anthropologists and folklorists, though our poetic sources only occasionally give us a tantalizing glimpse of this tradition. In the *Odyssey,* for example, Eumaios, while talking to the disguised Odysseus in his hut, casually refers to the pleasure, with food and drink at hand, of sharing tales of adventure, "when a man has had a life full of experience and wandering" (15.398–401). A poem of Xenophanes describes the same scene: "By the fireside in wintertime is when to speak of this, / when we are reclining on soft couches, full of food, / drinking sweet wine and munching chick peas: / 'Who are you among men? How many years ago was it, my good man— / how old were you?—when the Mede came?'" (F. 22 [Diels]).

Some people picture Herodotus as a famous world traveler who dazzled and delighted the crowds who thronged the festivals at Olympia with his readings. Others see him as a rustic from the provinces leaning in from the fringes of an elegant Athenian symposium to overhear a sophist's witty words. But if we imagine him seated at a fireside similar to that described by Xenophanes, we may gain our best glimpse of him as an artist: listening to stories, telling stories of his own, and collecting the stories of others. These tales have vanished for us but not utterly, for they live on in a new, written form and for a new purpose in the *Histories.*

One feature of the *Histories* that we can readily identify as a product of the anecdotal tradition is the attention and artistic effort Herodotus spends on individual details. Although his canvas is gigantic, Herodotus is essentially a miniaturist. It is at the level of the paragraph, the sentence, or even the choice of a single word that his subtlety is most apparent. Clearly, as we can see from such studies as Immerwahr's *Form and Thought,* Herodotus does try to organize the longer sections of his book, his *logoi,* in a consistent way with "proemial" statements to signal changes in topic; but few scholars would claim that organization of material on a large scale is one of Herodotus' strengths as a writer.

If we look beyond an organization by topic to organization by theme, however, we can see a higher level of artistry at work. Herodotus manages to break through the limited confines of the individual anecdote to transform an interesting story into a profound insight as he links a series of anecdotes that share a similar theme. A good example is the anecdote of the "clever, vengeful woman" and that of "excessive vengeance," which we examined in Chapter One. Here we encounter two interrelated themes, repeated in successive stories, that are the stock in trade of the racy, gossipy, interesting anecdote. But these themes are significant not just for brief narratives of isolated events but for the gigantic *logoi* of Xerxes' invasion and for the *Histories* as a whole. Perhaps unable to analyze the historical events about which he was writing, as a Thucydides might have done, Herodotus used the anecdotes to explain the meaning of those events for him. On the other hand, Herodotus' minute attention to the individual dramatic moments in anecdotes shows that, for him, history is made up of an infinite number of tiny, intricate details. He thus gives two focuses on the events he describes, a broad overview and an extreme close-up.

Another anecdotal feature of the *Histories* is that Herodotus only examines life's most intense moments. There is little of the everyday about the *Histories* because ordinary events do not make an anecdote interesting, even though the exceptional events described represent, by definition, only extraordinary and, thus, unrepresentative human experience. Herodotus is far from unaware of this paradox as we can see in his practice of telling conflicting factual and fictional versions of the same event. Rather than temper or soften this tendency of anecdotes to deal with extremes, Herodotus very characteristically tells stories that promote exactly opposite and contradictory ideas: one-man rule is best, but freedom is best, too. Here also anecdotes supply him with a model, and by examining this model we can explain a seemingly troublesome aspect of Herodotus' style.

In oral literature brief stories and anecdotes often make a concisely stated moral judgment based on the narrative, or they illustrate a particular ethical attitude. Since, however, such stories deal with extremes of human experience (stressing, for example, "the bravest," "the smallest," "the richest," or "the poorest"), they usually also represent extreme differences in moral outlook rather than subtle variations. For example, folktales often exhibit two contradictory attitudes to money and wealth. In one type of story, such as that of Jack and the Beanstalk, wealth is desirable and brings happiness. These stories reward their heroes with pots of gold and usually the hand of a beautiful—but certainly rich—princess. Yet in another type of story, a poor man learns to be satisfied with his poverty and not to yearn for more than he has. Wealthy kings, easily outmaneuvered by clever but impecunious heroes, appear only as the butt of jokes. In the Grimm collection, for example, the tale of the Fisherman's Wife teaches her that she does not really profit from having her wishes for money granted. The same ethical polarization in matters of morality occurs in folktales in general, as some stories celebrate traditional virtues of bravery, truthfulness, fidelity, or trustworthiness, but others heroize tricksters and rascals, who succeed by lying and cheating and who always evade punishment.[3]

Even when we move from the fictional world of folktales and fairy tales to legends and anecdotes about real people and actual events, we find a similar divergence in moral attitude. Most men around whom an anecdotal tradition has sprung up figure both as the hero and as the villain of those stories depending upon whether the source of a story was an admirer or an enemy. The more famous the man, the greater the extremes of opinion and the smaller likelihood of the survival of unbiased facts free from strong value judgments.

One kind of naive storyteller takes no notice of differences in moral outlook between one story or anecdote and another and makes no attempt at consistency but aims only to keep his audience entertained with one story after another. A second type of raconteur, however, does try to impose a unified point of view on his material and to present what he personally considers either factually or morally valid. In a literate society a narrator may make some effort to trace conflicting accounts back to their sources and to investigate their biases. But this is a difficult if not impossible task for a storyteller relying on oral tradition, in which, even if informants survive, versions will still differ. Moreover, universal story motifs quickly infiltrate accounts of historical events. Thucydides complains about his contemporaries (who are Herodotus' contemporaries as well): "Most of them are so uncritical in their pursuit of the truth," οὕτως ἀταλαίπωρος τοῖς πολλοῖς ἡ ζήτησις τῆς ἀληθείας (1.20). Even generations after Thucydides, historical writers who could have used documentary evidence to authenticate their accounts of the past turned instead to standard *topoi,* the literary descendants of moral motifs. Thus the choice of one of two oral traditions about past events or the choice of one moral position often represents only the whim of the storyteller rather than a search for truth or an opinion based on evidence.

Herodotus' portraits of the eastern monarchs provide an illustration of the contradictions that can arise when a writer conflates two oral traditions. All these kings, from Croesus to Xerxes, appear in some anecdotes as gentle and wise rulers, in others as cruel and stupid tyrants. There are some extremes, of course, for Herodotus tells more stories of the evil deeds of Cambyses than about other kings, but all the kings possess, to some degree, split personalities. The sources of these conflicting stories may be the actual noble or evil careers of the rulers, but their portraits may also have been influenced by traditions about other rulers. The sources could even lie in the characteristic legends and stories traditionally associated with all kings. In the oral traditions about their rules, even benign rulers will be charged with evil deeds while the most savage tyrants will show sporadic generosity. Although the storyteller who carefully selects and edits material to avoid inconsistencies may be less naive than one who arbitrarily tells all stories however contradictory, the former may omit and the latter include much evidence that is useful to the modern historian.

Opinions vary about the role of anecdotes in the *Histories.* For some, Herodotus is the naive raconteur of any good story, whether related to his subject or not. For such readers the stories Herodotus tells serve only as entertainment. Other readers recognize that the anecdotes present a consistent point of view, but they dismiss these stories as a series of clichés: "a moral and theological thicket of wealth and power and pride, and the downfall that comes to their possessors."[4] It has, moreover, often proved temptingly convenient for historians studying the period that Herodotus describes to discount the role of anecdotes in the *Histories.* To admit that Herodotus consciously, but without alerting the reader, weaves repeated fictional motifs throughout his book, attaching them to real characters and events, severely qualifies the confidence with which we can turn to him on every occasion as a historical source.

Yet what we might have lost in our confidence in Herodotus as a reliable source for historical information, we have gained in appreciation of him as an original writer and in fact creator of a unique genre. Herodotean scholarship has often focused, to Herodotus' detriment, on a comparison between some aspect of the *Histories* and another literary genre. The study of the "wise adviser," one of the first studies of a Herodotean motif, originated in an attempt to show the influence on Herodotus of the "tragic warner" of the Attic stage. Although such influences certainly exist and merit study, we need to look more today at Herodotus' innovative and original treatment of this material rather than at what he borrowed. There was "no Herodotus before Herodotus" and none afterward either. It is time to stop criticizing his work as a pastiche of other genres and explore the genre that he created.

Herodotus' originality lies in his variations of the same motif in parallel anecdotes. Thus he examines the same idea from a number of different and, in a characteristically Herodotean style, opposite and contradictory perspectives. The accumulated stories on the same theme ultimately give a subtle and complex range of views that transcends the potential impact of a single anecdote. Herodotus' implicit assumptions about anecdotes follow three of the major tenets of structuralist anthropology in its approach to myth in primitive cultures. First, the repeated stories and motifs that appear from a storytelling tradition reflect peoples' consciousness of human problems or situations inherently significant to their own culture. Second, the purpose of storytelling is often to mediate between irreconcilable opposites. Third, of stories that are continually repeated in variant versions, no one version is "correct" but all are "true" (even if the versions contradict each other), because all the versions speak to a culture's conception of its world.[5]

But Herodotus' book is not a random collection of naive stories by various tellers but the result of one man's thought. We can see a measure of his sophisticated outlook and both his similarities to and differences from primitive storytellers in the ways he varies the theme of the philosopher king. In folklore, stories of this type—a "wish fulfillment"—follow a stereotype: a young man of humble birth, through cleverness and often trickery and frequently with magical assistance, becomes king.[6] Sometimes he replaces a hated tyrant. Always he marries a beautiful princess and lives happily ever after, a ruler beloved by his people. Herodotus applies this model to the careers of both real and legendary kings, but unlike the storyteller, who intends only to amuse, Herodotus uses the stories of Deioces, Pisistratus, Darius, and Amasis to explore moral concerns never contemplated by the folkloric original. But, as in primitive traditions, no one of these kings represents Herodotus' idea of what is exactly right for a king to do or be, because they illustrate true alternatives for beneficial monarchies. A king may be a thoroughly good man like Deioces or a reprobate like Amasis, but still be a good king. But then Herodotus complicates this presentation by telling another group of stories that illustrate the opposite point: freedom is the most desirable human condition. One-man rule may be the best system of government, but men should have freedom, too. Herodotus, with an honesty and depth of perception usually denied him, acknowledges the complexity of human life and the lack of clear solutions to human problems.

Herodotus tried to understand his world by writing about it. An artist whose lifetime coincided with the end of oral and the beginning of written literature, he created a book that was unique to that moment and could never be repeated. To appreciate his achievement we must not only recognize its uniquely anecdotal nature but attempt to find a correct critical approach. My analysis of key contrary motifs in Herodotus' anecdotes is my attempt to suggest a new approach that accepts the work on its own terms in a way that—I would like to think—might have pleased its author.

ABBREVIATIONS

AC	*L'Antiquité Classique*
AHR	*American Historical Review*
AJP	*American Journal of Philology*
ASNP	*Annali della Scuola Normale Superiore di Pisa*
BCH	*Bulletin de Correspondance Hellénique*
CJ	*Classical Journal*
CP	*Classical Philology*
CQ	*Classical Quarterly*
CR	*Classical Review*
Eur.	Euripides
Jacoby, *FGrH*	Jacoby, F. *Fragmente der greichischen Historiker.* Berlin and Leiden, 1923–1958
von Fritz, *GG*	von Fritz, K. *Die griechische Geschichts-schreibung.* 2 vols. Berlin, 1967
G&R	*Greece and Rome*
GRBS	*Greek, Roman, and Byzantine Studies*

Hdt.	Herodotus
Hec.	Hecataeus
How and Wells	How, W. W., and J. Wells. *A Commentary on Herodotus.* 2 vols. Oxford, 1928, rpt. 1957
HSCP	*Harvard Studies in Classical Philology*
JARCE	*Journal of the American Research Center Egypt*
JHS	*Journal of Hellenic Studies*
JWI	*Journal of the Warburg and Courtauld Institutes*
LEC	*Les Études Classiques*
Legrand	Legrand, Ph.-E. *Hérodote: Histoires.* Paris, 1946–1956 [*Introduction, Index Analytique,* and 9 vols. of text and commentary]
Lexicon	Powell, J. E. *A Lexicon to Herodotus.* 2nd ed. Hildesheim, 1960
*LSJ*⁹	Liddell, H. G., R. Scott, and H. S. Jones. *A Greek-English Lexicon.* 9th ed. Oxford, 1953
Marg	Marg, W., ed. *Herodot: Eine Auswahl aus der neueren Forschung.* Wege de Forschung 26. 3rd ed. Darmstadt, 1982
MGR	*Miscellanea greca e romana*
Müller, *FHG*	Müller, C. *Fragmenta Historicorum Graecorum.* Paris, 1841–1870
MusAfr	*Museum Africum*
PAPhS	*Proceedings of the American Philosophical Society*
Pind.	Pindar
Plut.	Plutarch
PP	*La Parola del Passato*
QUCC	*Quaderni Urbinati di Cultura classica*
RE	*Paulys Real-Encyclopädie der classischen Altertumswissenschaft.* Edited by G. Wissowa et al. Stuttgart, 1884–

REA	*Revue des Études Anciennes*
REG	*Revue des Études Grecques*
RhM	*Rheinisches Museum*
Roscher, *Lexicon*	Roscher, W. H., ed. *Ausführliches Lexicon der griechischen und römischen Mythologie.* Leipzig, 1884–
Stein	Stein, H., ed. *Herodotos.* 9 vols. 1881–1896 and other dates, rpt. 9 vols. in 5. Zurich, 1962–1969
TAPA	*Transactions of the American Philological Association*
Thuc.	Thucydides
TLS	*Times Literary Supplement*
UCPCP	*University of California Publications in Classical Philology*
YCS	*Yale Classical Studies*

NOTES

Introduction

1. A. Momigliano, "The Place of Hdt. in the History of Historiography," in *Secondo contributo alla storia degli studi classici* (Rome, 1960) 31.
2. An extreme example of this division of the *Histories* into early and late passages can be found in J. E. Powell, *The History of Hdt.* (Cambridge, 1939).
3. "The work of Hdt. is richly furnished with these tales; he had a wonderful *flair* for a good story; and the gracious garrulity with which he tells historical anecdotes will secure him readers till the world's end." J. B. Bury, *Ancient Greek Historians* (New York, 1958) 57.
4. See H. Bischoff, *Der Warner bei Hdt.* (Leipzig, 1932), excerpts in Marg, 302–319; R. Lattimore, "The Wise Advisor in Hdt.," *CP* 34 (1939) 24–35.
5. See S. Flory, "Arion's Leap: Brave Gestures in Hdt.," *AJP* 99 (1978) 411–421. J. Cobet, *Hdt.'s Exkurse und die Frage der Einheit seines Werkes* (Weisbaden, 1971) and H. R. Immerwahr, *Form and Thought in Hdt.* (Cleveland, 1966) both take anecdotes seriously, though Cobet concentrates on the longer digressions and Immerwahr on the structure of the *Histories*.

6. For a critical analysis of the traditional view of Hdt.'s audience, see S. Flory, "Who Read Hdt.'s *Histories?*" *AJP* 101 (1980) 12–28.

7. R. Lattimore, "The Composition of the History of Hdt.," *CP* 53 (1958) 9–21.

8. See Flory, "Who Read Hdt.'s *Histories?*," esp. 28.

9. T. B. Macaulay, "History and Literature," in *Varieties of History,* ed. F. Stern (Cleveland, 1956) 78.

10. The book-length studies on Hdt., cited in the Bibliography, by Cobet, Immerwahr, Legrand (*Introduction*), Pohlenz, and Wood, however, all do give some valuable literary insights into specific passages. Of these, I think an English translation of Legrand would best serve the general English-speaking reader as an introduction to Hdt. The recently published book on Hdt. in the Twayne series by J. A. S. Evans (whose learning and knowledge of our author I admire) typically does not treat literary issues at all. The recent book by J. Hart, *Hdt. and Greek History* (London, 1982) shares this antiliterary bias.

11. See the Conclusion for more discussion of and references to literature on folktales.

12. K. H. Waters in *Hdt. the Historian* (Norman, 1985) refers to the *Histories* as the "Guinness Book of Records of the ancient world" (p. 7). In an otherwise comprehensive book, *Polarity and Analogy* (Cambridge, 1966), G. E. R. Lloyd cites no examples of polarity in Hdt., though he does cite several of analogy. A. B. Lloyd, on the other hand, calls Hdt.'s polarities "schematization" and treats this aspect of his thought as a weakness (*Hdt., Book II: Introduction,* Études préliminaires aux Religions orientales dans l'Empire Romain, vol. 43 [Leiden, 1975] 149–153). The best treatment of "opposites" so far is by Immerwahr, *Form and Thought,* 50–51, 234 n. 10 (the major Gk.-barbarian antitheses); 182–183, 262 (opposite actions); 321 (polarities in nature). The comprehensive nature of Immerwahr's book, however, and its focus on structure prevent him from treating these antitheses systematically. Cf. W. Schmid and O. Stählin, *Geschichte der griechischen Literatur* (Munich, 1934) 1.2.577–578 (Gk.-barbarian); 564 n. 1 (polarities in nature). H. Lloyd-Jones, *The Justice of Zeus* (Berkeley, 1971) calls the hardness-softness antithesis "far more fundamental" than the Greek-barbarian or liberty-despotism ones (p. 65).

13. On Hdt.'s "systematic oppositions" in the ethnographic sections of his book, see, most recently, J. Redfield, "Hdt. the Tourist," *CP* 80 (1985) 97–118, esp. 103–104.

14. On Xerxes' laughter see S. Flory, "Laughter, Tears, and Wisdom in Hdt.," *AJP* 99 (1978) 145–148.
15. First published in *Cornhill Magazine,* New Series 10 (1901) 444–445. On sophistical influences on Hdt., see A. Dihle, "Hdt. und die Sophistik," *Philologus* 106 (1962) 207–220, and W. Nestle, *Vom Mythos zum Logos* (Stuttgart, 1942; rpt. 1966) 503–505.
16. On Aeschylus' transformation of the cliché see A. Lebeck, *The Oresteia* (Cambridge, Mass., 1971) 173 n. 1.
17. "Herodotus" in *Oxford Classical Dictionary,* 2nd ed., p. 509. Cf. P. F. Pouncey, *The Necessities of War* (New York, 1980) 24. On Xerxes' contradictory actions, see Flory, "Laughter."
18. I owe this interpretation to Dr. Judith Binder of the American School of Classical Studies at Athens, delivered first on a memorable occasion in 1980 in the freezing January cold of the Acropolis Museum.

Chapter One. Logic and Accident

1. The best article on Thuc.'s "Archaeology" is by A. M. Parry, "Thuc.'s Historical Perspective," *YCS* 22 (1972) 49–61, esp. 53–56. See also Pouncey, *Necessities of War,* 43–53.
2. For a bibliography see H. Barth, "Zur Bewertung und Auswahl des Stoffes bei Hdt.," *Klio* 50 (1968) 93. The most detailed work is by H. Erbse, "Der Erste Satz im Werke Hdt.'s," in *Festschrift Bruno Snell* (Munich, 1956) 209–222. The intensity of scholarly interest in this first sentence has produced many categorical statements about its meaning (e.g., that ἔργα refers only to monuments [Jacoby, *RE* Sup. 2.333] or not at all to monuments [Legrand, 1.9–11]), but it has not greatly furthered our understanding of Hdt. For important work showing that αἰτία does not mean "cause" in a scientific or Aristotelian sense, however, see G. M. Kirkwood, "Thuc.'s Words for 'Cause,'" *AJP* 73 (1952) 37–61; L. Pearson, *"Prophasis* and *aitia,*" *TAPA* 83 (1952) 205–223; H. R. Immerwahr, "Aspects of Historical Causation in Hdt.," *TAPA* 87 (1956) 241–280; R. Sealey, "Thuc., Hdt., and the Causes of War," *CQ* 51 (1957) 1–12. Jacoby (*RE* 2.335) lays great emphasis on the τά τε ἄλλα καί that introduces the αἰτίην of the proemium as a crescendo device to introduce a concept that he believes crucial to the whole *Histories.* But τά τε ἄλλα καί is usually a *weak* connective phrase in Hdt. (e.g., 1.193.5; 2.127.1). Where emphatic, it is strengthened by other particles (e.g., 5.20.4 [καὶ δὴ καί], 6.136.1 [καὶ μάλιστα]). In the proemium, as in

7.9.1, I believe τά τε ἄλλα καί is a transition *only* to the immediately succeeding passage.

3. Scholars have seen in Hdt.'s opening chapters an attempt to distinguish absolutely between myth and history: M. Pohlenz, *Hdt.* (Stuttgart, 1961) 7–9; W. M. von Leyden, "Spatium Historicum," *Durham U. Jrnl.* 11 (1949–1950) 89–104, excerpts in Marg, 169–184; B. Shimron, "Πρῶτος τῶν ἡμεῖς ἴδμεν," *Eranos* 71 (1973) 45–51. But we must not expect Hdt. to be rigorous and consistent absolutely. Gyges is not his Adam. In her thought-provoking book, *Past and Process in Hdt. and Thuc.* (Princeton, 1982), V. Hunter argues that neither Hdt. nor Thuc. distinguishes between myth and history (pp. 93–107). I will treat this topic more fully in Chapter 2. For passages in Hdt. where elements of the *aitia* are treated as real, see 2.41 (Io); 1.173; 4.45, 147 (Europa); 4.179; 7.193 (the Argo and Jason); 7.62 (Medea). For the use of monuments to validate history, see H. R. Immerwahr, "*Ergon:* History as Monument in Hdt. and Thuc.," *AJP* 81 (1960) 261–290.

4. "If Hdt. could only have introduced his work with a few brief but pithy paragraphs like those in which Thuc. discussed the difficulty of establishing the truth and proclaimed his own zeal in ferreting it out, we should be likely to think much better of the father of history. But alas he actually commences with a faradiddle of woman stealing and thereafter never passes over an amazing or peculiar tale, unlikely though it may be" (C. G. Starr, *The Awakening of the Greek Historical Spirit* [New York, 1968] 142).

5. Here is a sampling of opinions as to why Hdt. rejects the *aitia:* because he does not believe in the "cherchez la femme" theory of history (J. L. Myres, *Hdt.: Father of History* [Oxford, 1953] 135–136); because he wants to outdo Hec. in unsentimentality (C. Fornara, *Hdt.: An Interpretative Essay* [Oxford, 1971] 20 n. 29); because he rejects the cold, alien attitude of "foreign scholars" to Greek myths (T. Gomperz, *Greek Thinkers,* tr. L. Magnus [London, 1901] 260); because of their Hecataean, naive certainty (W. Schadewaldt, "Hdt. als erster Historiker," *Die Antike* 10 [1934] 161; also in Marg, 113). Some scholars are not even sure Hdt. *does* reject the *aitia*. Pohlenz (*Hdt.,* 5–7) believes Hdt. is too fair-minded to pass judgment on the *aitia*. A. E. Wardman, "Hdt. on the Cause of the Greco-Persian Wars (Hdt., I.5)," *AJP* 82 (1961) 138, thinks Hdt. believes the events in the *aitia* occurred as related, but he thinks the historian dismisses them for their relative unimportance.

6. "I still fail to understand why Hdt. attributed stories that looked so obviously Greek to Phoenicians and Persians" (Momigliano, *Secundo contributo,* 14). Scholars have advanced widely diverging theories about the origins of the Persian *aitia,* often without reference to the theories of others. Some agree with Momigliano that the true source is Greek: D. Fehling, *Die Quellenangaben bei Hdt.: Studien zur Erzahlkunst Hdt.* (Berlin, 1971) 39–45; H. F. Bornitz, *Hdt.-Studien* (Berlin, 1968) 171–180. Others do believe Hdt. consulted Persian sources: K. Reinhardt, "Hdt.'s Persergeschichten," in *Vermächtnis der Antike,* ed. C. Becker (Göttingen, 1960) 133–174; also in Marg, 320–369; von Fritz, *GG* 1.166–167; J. Wells, *Studies in Hdt.* (Oxford, 1923) 95–111). For other specific theories: that the "Persian chroniclers" are actually Xanthus, see F. Altheim, *Literatur und Gesellschaft,* vol. 2 (Halle, 1950) 159–177; that they are actually Hec., see H. Diels, "Hdt. und Hekataios," *Hermes* 22 (1887) 411–444; that Hdt. was duped by a sophist who pretended to report Persian tales, see H. J. Rose, "Some Herodotean Rationalisms," *CQ* 34 (1940) 79; that Hdt. attributes the *aitia* to Persians in order to establish a "dispute," see Immerwahr, *Form and Thought,* 81; that Hdt. honestly reports from Asian sources "pénétrés du rationalisme ionien," see Legrand, 1.10; that the *aitia* later (7.43.1) allows Hdt. to present Xerxes as the avenger of Priam, see H. Montgomery, *Gedanke und Tat* (Stockholm, 1965) 13.

7. Chance has preserved the proemium of a book by Hec.: "Hec. the Milesian speaks as follows. I write about what I think is true, for in my opinion the Greeks tell many foolish stories" (F. 1, Jacoby, *FGrH*). For a general account with bibliography, see L. Pearson, *Early Ionian Historians* (Oxford, 1939).

8. See J. Wells, "Who Was Gyges?" in his *Studies in Hdt.* (Oxford, 1923) 19–26.

9. *Resp.* 2.359D. See K. Reinhardt, "Gyges und sein Ring," in *Vermächtnis der Antike,* ed. C. Becker (Göttingen, 1960) 175–183.

10. Nic. Dam. F. 47 (Jacoby, *FGrH* 2); F. 49 (Müller, *FHG* 3). See H. Diller, "Zwei Erzählungen des Lyders Xanthos," in *Navicula Chilonensis; Festschrift Jacoby,* (Leiden, 1956) 66–78.

11. I have learned much from the excellent article by H.-P. Stahl, "Hdt.'s Gyges-Tragödie," *Hermes* 96 (1968) 385–400, though I am not so convinced that drama influenced Hdt.'s style. For the most comprehensive treatment of the story and its variants, see K. F. Smith, "The Tale of Gyges and the King of Lydia I-II," *AJP* 23 (1902) 261–282, 362–387, and "The Literary Tradition of

Candaules and Gyges," *AJP* 41 (1920) 1–37. H. Erbse ("Tradition und Form im Werke Herodots," *Gymnasium* 68 [1961] 253–257) sees Hdt.'s Gyges story as a rationalization of the original of Plato's folktale, which the historian could not accept after scorning the Persian *aitia*. Closer to my own view is von Fritz, *GG* 1.224: "So hat Hdt. hier umgekehrt eine noch nich ganz zur eigentlichen Sage gewordene populäre geschichtliche Legende zur Dichtung gemacht." See also W. Aly, *Volksmärchen, Sage, und Novelle bei Hdt. und seinen Zeitgenossen* (Göttingen, 1921; rpt. 1969) 34–35, 228–230.

12. Stein explains the phrase ἠράσθη τῆς ἑωυτοῦ γυναικός as a prolepsis for ἠράσθη γυναικὸς καὶ ἔπειτα γήμας αὐτὴν ἐνόμιζε. But the parallel he cites (ἔγημε τὴν ἐρωμένην [3.31.6]) does not convince me that Hdt. is not here calling special attention to Candaules' peculiarly *helpless* passion. Cf. Eur. *Hipp.* 337 (of Pasiphaë). Legrand, too, seems to understate the case: "Le roi Candaule avait fait un mariage d'inclination."

13. On this phrase in Hdt. and on the writer's "mentalité archaïque," see the perceptive article by D. M. Pippidi, "Sur la philosophie de l'histoire d'Hdt.," *Eirene* 1 (1960) 75–92. P. Hohti, "Über die Notwendigkeit bei Hdt.," *Arctos* 9 (1975) 31–37, tries—unsuccessfully, I believe—to distinguish between divine and secular necessity in Hdt.

14. For the idea that Gyges violates the private, interior space held sacred by Greek families, see J. Gould, "Law, Custom, and Myth: Women in Classical Athens," *JHS* 100 (1980) 53–54. On *nomos* in general see M. Gigante, *Nomos Basileus* (Naples, 1956) and G. P. Shipp, *Nomos 'Law'* (Sydney, 1978).

15. The meaning of αἰδῶς in Gyges' maxim is much debated. A good bibliography may be found in H. Barth, "Nochmals Hdt. 1.8.3," *Philologus* 112 (1968) 288–291. For the most important earlier work, see R. Harder, "Hdt. 1.8.3," in *Studies Presented to D. M. Robinson II,* ed. G. E. Mylonas and D. Raymond (St. Louis, 1953) 446–449; also in Marg, 370–374. See now the excellent comments on this passage by M. Lang, *Herodotean Narrative and Discourse* (Cambridge, Mass., 1984) 37–51.

16. In the Greek there is a slight ambiguity: either she sees him as he goes out and sees that he is in the act of leaving or she only sees that he is in the room and does not see that—as it happens—he is leaving.

17. The bibliography on the Gyges fragment (*P. Oxy.* 23.2382) is

immense. Most recently see E. Bickel, "Rekonstruktions-Versuch einer hellenistischen Gyges-Nysia-Tragödie," *RhM* 100 (1957) 141–152. A key earlier article is A. Lesky, "Das hellenistische Gyges Drama," *Hermes* 81 (1953) 1–10.

18. A late Alexandrian grammarian (Ptolemaios Chennus, 1st c. A.D., Müller *FHG* 4, p. 278) preserves a delightful version in which Candaules' wife has double pupils and therefore can foil Gyges' ring of invisibility. It is Chennus also who tells us that Hdt. forbears to mention the name of Candaules' wife, Nisia, because it reminds him of the name of his own male lover, a recent suicide in an unhappy heterosexual affair!

19. See Flory, "Arion's Leap."

20. For analyses that stress Hdt.'s rationalism, see Rose, "Some Herodotean Rationalisms"; L. Pearson, "Credulity and Skepticism in Hdt.," *TAPA* 72 (1941) 333–355; Nestle, *Vom Mythos zum Logos,* 503–505; B. Baldwin, "How Credulous was Hdt.?" *G&R* 11 (1964) 167–177.

21. For possible influence of Heracleitus and other presocratics on Hdt., see Immerwahr, *Form and Thought,* 152–153, 324. Lloyd, *Polarity and Analogy,* 15–171, surveys polarity in the 5th c. and earlier but without reference to Hdt.

22. A. Salmon, "L'expérience de Psammétique," *LEC* 24 (1956) 321–329, believes Hdt. has here misinterpreted an anti-Psammetichean tall tale in which the pharaoh had the children raised by goats only to find that their first word was "baa!"

23. See Pearson, "Credulity and Skepticism."

24. See Immerwahr, *"Ergon."*

25. See Shimron, "Πρῶτος τῶν ἡμεῖς ἴδμεν," and von Leyden, "Spatium Historicum."

26. For other fatal banquets in Hdt. see 1.106 (Medes and Scythians), 2.121 (Rhampsinitus' treasure thief), 5.18 (Amyntas and the Persians). This motif reflects Hdt.'s feeling that pleasure and luxury are dangerous. I will return to this and related motifs in Chapters 3 and 4.

27. A fine article studies the close verbal parallels between the two stories: E. Wolff, "Das Weib des Masistes," *Hermes* 92 (1964) 51–58; also in Marg, 668–678.

28. Though she neither mentions Candaules' wife nor identifies revenge as a feminine trait, see the essential article by J. de Romilly, "La vengeance comme explication historique dans l'oeuvre d'Hdt.," *REG* 84 (1971) 314–337. The vengeance of Candaules'

wife closely resembles that of Astyages against Harpagus: delay, specificity, and bloodthirstiness (1.119ff.). But the lack of success of this revenge—for Harpagus ultimately, through Cyrus (1.124ff.), gets this revenge back—reveals his male stupidity. Harpagus' own masculine revenge is also incomplete, since Cyrus denies him credit for inspiring the revolt (1.129).

29. S. Luria, "Frauenpatriotismus und Sklavenemanzipation," *Klio* 26 (1933) 211–228, discusses—though not in this passage in Hdt.— the motif of female over male as a byword for topsy-turvydom. If Luria is correct, Hdt. here inverts the proverb by having a usually positive omen forebode ill.

30. Philip Slater, *The Glory of Hera* (Boston, 1968).

Chapter Two. Truth and Fiction

1. The classic accusation that Hdt. is a liar applies to his description of Babylon and appears in A. H. Sayce, *The Ancient Empires of the East* (London, 1883) xxix–xxxiii. Modern research, however, shows Hdt. to have been a fairly accurate *observer*. See O. E. Ravn, *Hdt.'s Description of Babylon,* tr. M. Tovberg-Jensen (Copenhagen, 1942). A recent series of articles by O. K. Armayor once again accuses Hdt. of describing what he has not seen: "Did Hdt. Ever Go to the Black Sea?" *HSCP* 82 (1978) 45–62; "Did Hdt. Ever Go to Egypt?" *JARCE* 15 (1980) 59–71; "Sesostris and Hdt.'s Autopsy of Thrace, Colchis, Inland Asia Minor, and the Levant," *HSCP* 84 (1980) 51–74. A. J. Podlecki, "Hdt. in Athens?" in *Greece and the Eastern Mediterranean: Studies Presented to F. Schachermeyr on the Occasion of His Eightieth Birthday,* ed. K. H. Kinzl (Berlin, 1977) 246–265, even suggests Hdt. may never have visited Athens. Pearson, "Credulity and Skepticism," esp. 339, stresses the historian's disregard for truth in the interests of keeping his audience entertained. Baldwin, "How Credulous was Hdt.?" emphasizes Hdt.'s skepticism. Despite their interest, these last two articles confuse two issues that I think can and should be kept separate: the historian's acuity as an observer and his (ironic or naive?) credulity in telling stories and anecdotes. See also J. A. S. Evans, "Father of History and Father of Lies; The Reputation of Hdt.," *CJ* 64 (1968) 11–17 and J. R. Grant, "Some Thoughts on Hdt.," *Phoenix* 37 (1983) 283–298.

2. W. Luther, "Der frühgriechische Wahrheitsgedanke im Lichte der Sprache," *Gymnasium* 65 (1958) 75–107, esp. 77, discusses the terminology (e.g., ἀλήθεια = "Unverborgenheit" ["the quality of

not being hidden"]). C. R. Ligota, "Fact and Fiction in Antiquity," *Journal of the Warburg and Courtauld Institutes* 45 (1982) 1–13, notes the low priority of facts in ancient historiography. Cf. M. I. Finley, "Myth, Memory, and History," in his *The Use and Abuse of History* (London, 1975) 11–33; also in *History and Theory* 4 (1965) 281–302: "Truth . . . was neither an important consideration nor a claim one could substantiate" (29). See also G. Schepens, "L'idéal de l'information complète chez les historiens grecs," *REG* 88 (1975) 81–93, which summarizes L. Canfora, *Totalità e selezione nella storiografia classica* (Bari, 1972) and C. G. Starr, "Ideas of Truth in Early Greece," *PP* 23 (1968) 348–359.

3. Thuc. seems to describe a kind of truth (τὰ δέοντα) differing from literal truth, when he says of the speeches in his work: ὡς δ'ἂν ἐδόκουν ἐμοὶ ἕκαστοι περὶ τῶν αἰεὶ παρόντων τὰ δέοντα μάλιστ' εἰπεῖν ἐχόμενῳ ὅτι ἐγγύτατα τῆς ξυμπάσης γνώμης τῶν ἀληθῶς λεχθέντων, οὕτως εἴρηται (1.22.1).

4. See G. Kennedy, *The Art of Persuasion in Greece* (Princeton, 1963) 58–60 and 99–100.

5. My interpretation of the Hesiod passage follows in some respects that of P. Pucci, *Hesiod and the Language of Poetry* (Baltimore, 1977) 9–16. See also G. P. Edwards, *The Language of Hesiod in Its Traditional Context* (Oxford, 1971) 167–168.

6. See E. A. Havelock, *Preface to Plato* (Oxford, 1963) 104–105.

7. For an analysis of Odysseus' guileful lies here, see W. J. Woodhouse, *The Composition of Homer's Odyssey* (Oxford, 1930) 129–131.

8. For a discussion of the rationalism of Hec. (with bibliography), see R. Drews, *The Greek Accounts of Eastern History* (Washington, D.C., 1973) 16–18. The usual view, represented by T. S. Brown in "Hdt. and his Profession," *AHR* 59 (1954) 829–843, esp. 841, is that Hdt. apes the rationalism of Hec.

9. Drews, *The Greek Accounts,* esp. 66–67, gives a useful analysis of the chronological relation of the Persian wars to Hdt.'s lifetime and the significance of this relation for Hdt.'s writing.

10. On this motif and especially the crossing of the Hellespont, see H. R. Immerwahr, "Historical Action in Hdt.," *TAPA* 85 (1954) 19–27.

11. On the question of the plausibility of this narrative, see A. Maude and J. L. Myres, "The Desert Pipe-line in Hdt. 3.9," *CR* 60 (1946) 19.

12. Note, too, that Cambyses receives advice from a certain Phanes and the help of the Arabian king in crossing the desert (3.4). The

sea captain is not the only wise adviser whose life hangs in the balance, for Croesus narrowly escapes the wrath of Cambyses (3.36). Lattimore, "The Wise Advisor," does not list Xerxes' captain among the "Practical Advisors" (26–28), but surely he belongs there.

13. Hdt. does not doubt that Cyrus punished the river Gyndes by dividing it into multiple channels (1.189–190). On the other hand, the story of Skyllias (8.8) follows the pattern of the three water-boundary stories exactly, though since Skyllias is a diver, he crosses the boundary by going *under* it. Hdt. describes this remarkable dive but then says he thinks Skyllias actually went by boat!

14. The best treatment of Xerxes' behavior in this anecdote and generally is by Immerwahr in *Form and Thought,* 182–183: "Xerxes rewards and punishes his own subjects to excess. He honors and respects certain sanctuaries but destroys others." Aly, *Volksmärchen,* 87, finds Xerxes' character here "Typus des echten Sultans." S. Benardete, *Herodotean Inquiries* (Hague, 1969) 4–5, finds the whole anecdote a "caricature of justice."

15. Hdt. gives a particularly gruesome example of the Persian acquiescence to their king in Prexaspes' response when Cambyses shoots his son through the heart: "Sire, I do not think god himself could shoot so well" (3.35). Hdt.'s use of the word for "taste," γεύω, reveals the pattern of happiness soon followed by disaster. In the *Histories,* characters usually get a brief taste of something good before suffering disaster (1.71; 4.147; 6.5; 7.46).

16. R. W. Macan, *Hdt.: The Seventh, Eighth, and Ninth Books* (London, 1908): "Persian grandees would have been but sorry hands at the oars compared with the Phoenician tars, and the process of pitching a lot of oarsmen into the sea during a raging storm to make room for the aristocratic amateurs might not have been easy or expeditious." See similar complaints about Hdt.'s logic in How and Wells, and in Legrand (8.119).

17. G. Rawlinson, *History of Hdt.* (London, 1875; many subsequent reprints).

18. F. J. Groten, Jr., "Hdt.'s Use of Variant Versions," *Phoenix* 17 (1963) 79–87. Groten's selective citations and insensitivity to Herodotean irony allow him to say (p. 79): "[Hdt.] feels an obligation to report what is reported to him (7.152.3), to record what all manner of people told him just as they told it (2.123.1), although he may not believe it (7.152.3)."

19. For example, Baldwin ("How Credulous was Hdt.?" 175) writes: "I think I have amply demonstrated how cautious Hdt. is in accepting native traditions, how he rejects some, accepts others, and, when in doubt, sets down the alternative versions for his readers to decide." von Fritz (*GG* 1.419–20) recognizes that Hdt. is inconsistent in his selectivity and inclusiveness, but he attributes this to traces in the *Histories* of earlier uncritical stages in Hdt.'s development as a writer. Rose ("Some Herodotean Rationalisms," 78) represents an opposite view of a naive Hdt. when he admits that there are in the *Histories* many stories that the writer found "incredible, but too good to be omitted." Plut. (*de Herodoti malignitate* 855E) complains that when Hdt. can choose between two or more versions, he always chooses "the nastier," τῷ χείρονι.

20. This concentration on Book Two weakens the otherwise interesting work on Hdt. by Hunter (*Past and Process*).

21. One hitherto unnoticed peculiarity of Book Two is that Hdt. refers to himself in the first-person singular much more often than elsewhere.

22. As in the case of the prophetic procedure among the Satrai—not to mention the procedure at Delphi—Hdt. sometimes clearly does not tell all he knows. For religious scruples, as is well known, Hdt. forbears to mention the name of Osiris, on which see I. M. Linforth, "Hdt.'s Avowal of Silence in His Account of Egypt," *UCPCP* 7 (1924) 269–292. See also R. Ball, "Hdt.'s List of the Spartans Who Died at Thermopylae," *MusAfr* 5 (1976) 1–8. Ball argues that Hdt. did not want to bore an Athenian audience with such a list.

23. We can observe the same phenomenon in the devaluation in meaning of such English words as "incredible" and "unbelievable." If there were truly no chance of convincing anyone of the fine taste of an ice cream that is advertised as "incredibly delicious," the advertising firm (and its clients) would soon be out of business.

24. Similarly, though King Midas of Phrygia is only a name in the *Histories* (1.14, 35, 45; 8.138), it seems hard to believe Hdt. had heard no stories about him, given the richness of the examples collected (e.g., in Roscher's *Lexicon*).

25. For other themes in this story see Flory, "Laughter," 149–150.

26. On this motif see Flory, "Arion's Leap," 411–421.

27. Hdt. tells another story of the triumph of a youngest son through

magical means (8.137). On this Märchen motif in Hdt. see Aly, *Volksmärchen,* 116, 196–197; for the motif generally, see Stith Thompson, *Motif-Index of Folk-Literature,* rev. ed. (Bloomington, 1979) H 1242, M 312.2.2

28. Hdt.'s practice of telling embarrassing alternative versions may have influenced Tacitus. For Tacitus' style of telling story variants, see I. S. Ryberg, "Tacitus' Art of Innuendo," *TAPA* 73 (1942) 383–404.

29. These are the usual verbs in Greek for dropping and weighing anchor. See *LSJ⁹*.

30. See G. L. Cooper, III, "Intrusive Oblique Infinitives in Hdt.," *TAPA* 104 (1974) 23–76.

31. Stein suggests that Hdt.'s story comes from a skolion. If so, the irreverence of Attic symposia about heroes of the Persian wars confirms what Thuc. has the Athenians say: τὰ δὲ Μηδικὰ καὶ ὅσα αὐτοὶ ξύνιστε, εἰ καὶ δι' ὄχλου μᾶλλον ἔσται αἰεὶ προβαλλομένα, ἀνάγκη λέγειν (1.73.2; cf. 1.86.1; 2.35).

32. Where Hdt. does use the word ἀτρεκέως of his own knowledge, in more than 90 percent of the cases the usage is negative (Hdt. is "*not* unerringly sure"). See Powell's *Lexicon.*

33. In the corpus and in Homer the usage of ἀτρεκέως is usually positive (cf. note 32 above). Hdt. mimics Homer's positive usage, however, at 7.47: φέρε τοῦτό μοι ἀτρεκέως εἰπέ.

34. We may identify here a Herodotean motif of the "king's research." Similarly, Cyrus conducts an experiment to see if the Persians are willing to revolt against the Medes (1.125–126), Darius establishes (through a questionnaire) that "*nomos* is king over all" (3.38), and Darius also sponsors voyages of discovery (4.44).

35. Hdt. elsewhere shows his willingness (though not without a sly wink) to admit the respectability and importance of prostitution in many cultures. The Lydians prostitute their daughters in order to gain dowries (1.93). The pyramid of Mycerinus' daughter would not be the first major monument raised by prostitutes' wages, since prostitutes made the largest donation toward the tomb of Alyattes (1.93).

Chapter Three. Nature and Culture

1. Most scholars follow J. Jüthner, *Hellenen und Barbaren* (Leipzig, 1923) 13–21, in attributing the growth of the pejorative meaning

to the Persian wars. See *Grecs et Barbares,* Fondation Hardt, En-tretiens 8 (Vandoeuvres, Genève, 1961), particularly the papers by H. Schwabl, "Das Bild der fremden Welt bei den frühen Griechen" (1–36) and H. Diller, "Die Hellenen-Barbaren An-tithese im Zeitalter der Perserkrieg" (39–82). The word first oc-curs in Greek prose in Heracleitus (F 107) and is clearly pe-jorative. A fundamental article by I. Weiler, "Greek and Non-Greek World in the Archaic Period," *GRBS* 9 (1968) 21–29, argues that even before the Persian wars and even in Homer there is a "Distanzgefühl" between Greek and barbarian.

2. Hdt.'s usage of the word in its most pejorative sense (i.e., "cruel," "uncivilized"), however, appears to be limited to a single passage: λέγειν βάρβαρα τε καὶ ἀτάσθαλα (7.35.2). Some other passages, however, are ambiguous.

3. Plut., *de Hdt. malig.* 857A, cf. 867C. A work called Περὶ τοῦ καταψεύσθαι τὴν Ἡροδότου ἱστορίαν by Aelius Harpokration is cited in the Suda. Similar works are discussed in Schmid and Stählin, *Geschichte der griechischen Literatur,* 1.2, 665–670. See the brilliant discussion by Momigliano on the reluctance in antiq-uity even among Hdt.'s advocates to argue that he did not tell lies: "The Place of Herodotus," esp. 29–30 and 35–36 in *Secondo contributo.*

4. For Hdt.'s development see von Fritz, *GG* 1, 419–420. H. C. Avery, "Hdt.'s Picture of Cyrus," *AJP* 93 (1972) 529–546, argues that the two-sided picture of Cyrus is a deliberate "model or exemplar" (529) illustrating character disintegration, and that Hdt. "was in control of his material" (530). I am greatly in sympa-thy with the approach and some of the conclusions of T. Spath, *Das Motiv der doppelten Beleuchtung bei Hdt.* (Vienna, 1968), who treats the "Hellenen und Barbaren" antithesis (254–262); but he prejudices his case here and generally by giving a superficial and brief treatment of too many different "double illuminations." I also feel Spath mistakenly overlooks the strong polarity of Hdt.'s views of Athens. See also the excellent review article by H. Ver-din, "Hdt. historien? Quelques interprétations récentes," *AC* 44 (1975) 668–685. From among the many scholars who resist at-tempts to analyze literary patterns, even patterns of contradiction, I cite the remark of K. H. Waters: "It is in my opinion an error to impose upon Herodotus 'a pattern'. . . . He was too much of a realist to think that all historical events conformed to one type of pattern, and too good a literary artist to have filled his work with

repetitive themes even if the literary aspect had in fact predomi-
nated over the historical." "Hdt. and the Ionian Revolt," *Historia*
19 (1970) 505.

5. For general accounts of the range of meaning of the term, see H.
Bacon, *Barbarians in Greek Tragedy* (New Haven, 1961); V.
Ehrenberg, *The People of Aristophanes* (Oxford, 1951) 147–154;
and A. Diller, *Race Mixture Among the Greeks Before Alexander*
(Urbana, 1937) 14–56. In the Fondation Hardt discussion (see
note 1 above) of Diller's talk, H. C. Baldry notes that the Greeks
encountered barbarians on Greek soil as slaves and not on the
frontiers in their own habitats (75–76). This circumstance might
account for many of the negative images of barbarians in tragedy
and comedy.

6. For a collection of passages in Greek literature describing noble
savages, see A. O. Lovejoy and G. Boas, *Primitivism and Related
Ideas in Antiquity* (Baltimore, 1935) 287–367. Hdt.'s treatment
of the noble savage is perhaps the most detailed and is frequently
mentioned, but it has not been studied in detail. For example, see
G. Murray, *Greek Studies* (Oxford, 1946) 55: "He has a romantic
admiration for the Scythians and other *Natürvolker* as Tacitus has
for the Germans." But see also the brief discussion by Cobet,
Hdt.'s Exkurse, 111–116, of the "primitive Gegner" theme.

7. Of the ten times Hdt. uses the adjective ἀξιοθέητος, "worth
looking at" (*Lexicon*), six are in association with measurements or
statistics or are a general comment about size (1.184; 2.111, 163,
176.1, 176.2; 4.85).

8. For an account of Hdt.'s sympathy with Polycrates, see V. La Bua,
"Logos samio e storia samia in Erodoto," *MGR* 6 (1978) 1–88.

9. We find here a revealing example of Hdt.'s "dislocated additions,"
for which see Lattimore, "The Composition of the History," esp.
12, where this passage is noted. Because of the awkwardness of
inserting corrections in a manuscript in Hdt.'s day, the writer adds
the extra detail about the decoration of the spears held downward
by soldiers in front of Xerxes when he thinks of it, not a few
sentences earlier "where it logically belongs." I would only add to
Lattimore's excellent analysis that the question here is also one of
Hdt.'s taste, revealed in his addition of an extra symmetrical
detail.

10. Commonly, however, scholars attribute the details of the catalogue to a written source rather than to Hdt.'s imaginative desire
for variety; see, for example, How and Wells (7.61): "The ultimate authority must be official Persian documents." Cf. G. B.

Grundy, *The Great Persian War* (London, 1901) 219: "To take [the catalogue] in detail would be wearisome, and is unnecessary. . . . [It is] probable that the list is founded on information culled from Ionian geographers."

11. It is tempting to suppose either that Hdt.'s source for the catalogue was a frieze or tapestry (with names embroidered after the fashion of ceramic art) or that he was inspired by the style of such works of art to create this singular description. For a case where art may have inspired Hdt., see V. Massaro, "Hdt.'s Account of the Battle of Marathon and the Picture in the Stoa Poikile," *AC* 47 (1978) 458–475.

12. On this episode as a *topos,* see F. H. Stubbings, "Xerxes and the Plane Tree," *G&R* 15 (1946) 63–67.

13. For other motifs in the story of Xerxes at Abydos, see Flory, "Laughter," esp. 146–147.

14. The catalogue of Xerxes' army includes primitive tribes such as Scythians and Ethiopians who are considered to be noble savages elsewhere in the *Histories.* But in this context, despite their often primitive equipment, they constitute part of the wealth of the prosperous aggressor.

15. A fragment of Aeschylus (196) refers to certain Gabii, who may be the same as Homer's Abii. Cf. Fr. 198, where the Scythians are called εὔνομοι. For the Cyclopes see G. S. Kirk, *The Nature of Greek Myths* (Harmondsworth, 1974) 85–86.

16. For the terminology "hard" and "soft," see Lovejoy and Boas, *Primitivism,* 10.

17. For the Hyperboreans see esp. Pind., *Pyth.* 10.30–36 and Lovejoy and Boas, *Primitivism,* 305.

18. Paradoxically, the only other place where Hdt. uses ἁβρός is to call the Scythians, noble savages, ἁβρότατοι (4.104) because they wear gold jewelry in quantity. But gold, although a sign of the wealth of prosperous aggressors, is also a metal easily worked by primitive peoples without the use of elaborate smelting. Gold, like milk, is therefore a "primitive" substance.

19. For "tasting" in Hdt. see Chapter 2, note 15.

20. A. T. Olmstead, *History of the Persian Empire* (Chicago, 1948) 22–23, 34–41.

21. A. Bovon, "La représentation des guerriers perses et la notion de barbare dans la 1ʳᵉ moitié du Vᵉ siècle," *BCH* 87 (1963) 579–602.

22. Wine, like gold, is an ambivalent sign of civilization, as anthropologists of the structuralist school have taught us. Wine

represents higher civilization because its production requires patience and sophistication (in structuralist terms, it is "cooked"). But wine is also a natural ("raw") product. In Greek society wine also has associations of restrained culture (the dignified symposium) and of chaos (the wild drunkenness of the centaurs). See also H. Usener, "Milch und Honig," *RhM* 57 (1902) 177–195, and the splendid article by M. Rossellini and S. Saïd, "Usages des femmes et autres *nomoi* chez les 'sauvages' d'Hérodote: essai de lecture structurale," *ASNP* 8 (1978) 949–1005.

23. See J. A. S. Evans, "The Dream of Xerxes and the 'Nomoi' of the Persians," *CJ* 57 (1961) 109–111.

24. What the Persians have imported from abroad are chiefly their luxurious habits (εὐπαθείας) among which Hdt. singles out pederasty (παισὶ μίσγονται), learned, he slyly claims, from the Greeks (1.135).

25. Though I admire the elegant analysis of H.-P. Stahl, "Learning through Suffering? Croesus' Conversations in the History of Hdt.," *YCS* 24 (1975) 1–36, I strongly disagree with his conclusion that Croesus' advice is flawed because he does not consider what will happen if Tomyris wins on her side of the river. Croesus does not explicitly analyze this case for Cyrus because of a sense of delicacy, but he clearly has thought out all possible outcomes.

26. Many of the traits of Hdt.'s noble savages appear to be deliberately contrived opposites (and thus criticisms) of the corresponding Greek customs. This is noted by H. C. Baldry, *The Unity of Mankind in Greek Thought* (Cambridge, 1965) 21, and forms a major theme of F. Hartog, *Le miroir d'Hdt.: Essai sur la représentation de l'autre* (Paris, 1980).

27. The Massagetae make no later appearance in the *Histories* as either vassals or rulers of another state.

28. Meat-eating is usually understood to be a sign of disintegration from an earlier utopian state. See J. Ferguson, *Utopias of the Classical World* (London, 1975) 18. Though the Ethiopians are meat eaters, their "table" frees them from the necessity of actually slaughtering animals. See J. P. Vernant, "Les troupeaux du soleil et la table du soleil," *REG* 85 (1972) xiv–xvii.

29. Hdt.'s conception of the noble savage, like ours of the American Indian, seems to involve men who fight with bow and arrow (often from horseback). For a clever linguistic argument that the Ethiopians were first known as possessors of long bows (βιοί) not long lives (βίοι), see H. Last, ΑΙΘΙΟΠΕΣ ΜΑΚΡΟΒΙΟΙ, *CQ* 17 (1923) 35–36.

30. See Ehrenberg, *The People of Aristophanes,* 175.
31. For this "brave gesture" see Flory, "Arion's Leap."
32. Cf. Sext. Emp., *adv. math.* 2.23. My interpretation of this passage confirms that of Stein and Legrand rather than that of How and Wells. Cf. the Spartan ephor, Sthenelaidas, at Thuc., 1.86.1: τοὺς μὲν λόγους τοὺς πολλοὺς τῶν 'Αθηναίων οὐ γιγνώσκω, and his inability to understand the shouted votes of the Spartans (he wants them to act out their votes silently by a "division of the house").
33. See F. Hartog, "Les amazones d'Hdt.: Inversions et tiers exclus," in *Pour Leon Poliakov: Le racisme. Mythes et Sciences,* ed. M. Olender (Paris and Brussels, 1981) 177–186. See also works by Lefkowitz, Pembroke, Rossellini and Saïd, and Tyrrell cited in the Bibliography.
34. One set of relationships that does not quite fit this pattern is Persia's conquest of Babylon and Egypt. Nevertheless, Persia's status as a noble savage (because, relative to these more ancient civilizations, she is a noble savage) explains her victory in these cases.
35. See Vernant, "Les troupeaux du soleil," xvii.
36. See Rossellini and Saïd, "Usages des femmes," 955.
37. The weakness of Asiatics like the Ionians looms large in the mind of the author of the Hippocratic essay Περὶ 'Αέρων 'Υδάτων Τόπων (12, 16). This writer seems more prejudiced against the East than Hdt., though understandably he stresses weakness and disease rather than the robust health of the noble savage. For him the Scythians are fat, slothful, and effeminate (17). The bravery of *some* European tribes he treats only summarily (24).

Chapter Four. Freedom and Discipline

1. How and Wells, 2: 338. Cf., e.g., Fornara, *Hdt.,* 48–50. For more balanced views, see J. N. Davie, "Hdt. and Aristophanes on Monarchy," *G&R* 26 (1979) 160–168 and W. G. Forrest, "Hdt. and Athens," *Phoenix* 38 (1984) 1–11.
2. See *Lexicon,* s. vv. Cf. A. Andrewes, *The Greek Tyrants* (London, 1956) 27. My disagreement with A. Ferrill, "Hdt. on Tyranny," *Historia* 27 (1978) 385–398, will be obvious.
3. The usual conclusion of scholarly treatments of these three passages is that Hdt. passes on sophistic (Protagorean?) diatribes he has overheard. See K. Stroheker, "Zu den Anfängen der monar-

chischen Theorie in der Sophistik," *Historia* 2 (1953–1954) 381–
412. Cf. T. B. L. Webster, *Political Interpretations in Greek Literature* (Manchester, 1948) 49–50. On the Conspirators' Debate,
see, most recently, J. A. S. Evans, "Notes on the Debate of the
Persian Grandees in Hdt.," *QUCC* 36 (1981) 69–84.

4. For a general account of the connotations of "tyrant," see Andrewes, *The Greek Tyrants,* 21–23. More detailed discussion with
bibliography may be found in R. Drews, "The First Tyrants in
Greece," *Historia* 21 (1972) 129–144.

5. How and Wells. Cf. G. Grote, *A History of Greece* (London, 1869)
231: "despot's progress." But Grote's account, one of the most
sympathetic (229–232), does connect Deioces with the Conspirators' Debate. The story of Deioces has not attracted attention.
Most see it as a reflection of sophistic ideas rather than Hdt.'s own
opinion. See Stroheker, "Zu den Anfängen," 385–386.

6. See Myres, *Hdt.,* 54–55: "[Deioces] fell in love with power . . . till he attained this freedom of action and could impose his
abnormal will on his neighbors."

7. The only other time Hdt. uses αὐτόνομος (8.140α2), it clearly
means "independently governed," but in its context here it refers
not to the Medes' liberation from the Assyrians but to their individual style of life.

8. To my knowledge, this pun has never been noted. For the ety-
mological connection between the Greek word for "tyranny" and
"judging," see A. J. Podlecki, "Festivals and Flattery: The Early
Greek Tyrants as Patrons of Poetry," *Athenaeum* 58 (1980) 374–
375. Hdt. is fond of pun names, e.g., Ἄδρηστος (1.35), Φύη
(1.60), Τιμόδημος (8.125).

9. For the Athenians' modest private houses, see Dem. 3.25. For
their abandonment of the practice of bearing arms, see Thuc. 1.6.
The possession of spear bearers was a particular mark of an oriental king. In arguing that the boy Cyrus has actually "ruled" over
his playmates, Astyages' priest stresses that he had "spear bearers,
door-keepers, and message carriers" (1.120.2). For a comparison
of Greek and oriental cities, see V. Ehrenberg, *The Greek State*
(Oxford, 1960) 3: "The cities of the East . . . found their center
in the royal palace; such a center is not to be found among the
later Greeks even while there were kings."

10. See note 8 above and J. E. Powell, "Puns in Hdt.," *CR* 51 (1937)
103–105. Powell, however, does not notice these particular puns.

11. I take Hdt.'s statement (1.60.3) that the Hellenes have always

been "smarter and more free from foolishness" than the barbarians as ironic. But an emendation suggested by W. Burkert, "Iranisches bei Anaximandros," *RhM* 106 (1963) 97–98, would make the text read that actually the *barbarians* were smarter.

12. Although Pisistratus is once again exiled, Hdt. concludes the narrative of the accession of the Athenian tyrant with a catalogue of his good deeds (1.64), thus following the same organization as with Darius and Psammetichus.

13. To my knowledge Darius' duplicity at this point in the narrative has not been noted. If I am right in my interpretation, Darius resembles Amasis, another spur-of-the-moment usurper (2.162.2), who soon admits to having been planning his rebellion for a long time (2.162.4).

14. For the use of ἰσονομία for "democracy," see M. Ostwald, *Nomos and the Beginnings of Athenian Democracy* (Oxford, 1969) 111–113.

15. Considerable uncertainty about the meaning of the debate prevails. For the idea that Otanes' speech refers to Athens, see G. Hirst, "Hdt. on Tyranny *versus* Athens and Democracy," in her *Collected Classical Papers* (Oxford, 1938) 97–110, esp. 104. For the idea that Hdt. implicitly sympathizes with Otanes' arguments, see D. Kagan, *The Great Dialogue: The History of Greek Political Thought from Homer to Polybius* (New York, 1965) 69: "We must, I believe, reject immediately the possibility that Hdt. supports the argument for monarchy." For the idea that the argument for monarchy conceals an apologia for Perikles' position in Athens, see J. S. Morrison, "The Place of Protagoras in Athenian Public Life," *CQ* 35 (1941) 1–16, esp. 12–13. Hdt. is usually presumed to be friendly to Athens, but this idea is strenuously attacked by H. Strasburger, "Hdt. und das perikleische Athen," *Historia* 4 (1955) 1–25. The idea is, however, defended again by F. D. Harvey, "The Political Sympathies of Hdt.," *Historia* 15 (1966) 254–255.

16. See Burkert, "Iranisches bei Anaximandros." In another revealing passage Hdt. describes how a certain Lykidas is stoned to death for suggesting that Persian peace proposals be put before "the people," τὸν δῆμον (9.5), presumably because of the untrustworthiness of that unruly body.

17. Cf. the story of Zopyrus (3.153–158), who receives a divine sign *first* and then contrives the fall of Babylon through purely human ingenuity.

18. See 1.99: ὁρᾶσθαι βασιλέα ὑπὸ μηδενός.
19. For the absence of Egyptian records, see, e.g., How and Wells. The connection between this passage and the Conspirators' Debate and the suggestion of sophistic influence have not, to my knowledge, been noted before.
20. The prophecy puts the oligarchs into a situation common in folktales and exemplified by the motif of the "Unique Prohibition": the hero is forbidden to do one thing, but all else he is free to do. See Stith Thompson, *Motif-Index,* C 600. If the narrative has a specific origin in folklore, it is tempting to posit a version in which the oligarchs remained constantly together to keep one another under observation and to prevent fulfillment of the prophecy.
21. Another king who possibly acts the part of wise adviser is Thrasyboulus (5.92ζ), but his advice, which is wordless, hardly compares with the eloquence of Amasis.
22. Amasis' mixture of respect and cynicism in testing oracles contrasts with the naiveté of Croesus' tests of the oracles (1.46–49). One doubts if the shrewd Amasis would have been deceived by a misleading oracle.
23. Because of the many contacts between Amasis and the Greeks, which Hdt. himself records (2.178–182), we may imagine that there was a rich store of anecdotes about Amasis from which Hdt. could choose. Diodorus Siculus apparently follows Hdt. but censors the portrait of Amasis by making him wealthy and prominent (1.67–68).
24. See Strasburger, "Hdt. und das perikleische Athen," and Podlecki, "Hdt. in Athens?"
25. See Flory, "Laughter," and D. Lateiner, "A Note on the Perils of Prosperity in Hdt.," *RhM* 125 (1982) 97–101.
26. The usual interpretation of Hdt.'s account of Samos and Polycrates is that it illustrates the evils of tyranny. See H. R. Immerwahr, "The Samian Stories of Hdt.," *CJ* 52 (1957) 312–322, esp. 322: "The Samians are an important example of the struggle between freedom and slavery which is a fundamental theme in Hdt.'s work."

Conclusion. Anecdotes and History

1. The *Oxford English Dictionary* gives the following definition: "The narrative of a detached incident or of a single event, told as being in itself interesting or striking. (*At first,* an item of gossip.)"

2. I have learned much from H. White, "The Question of Narrative in Contemporary Historical Theory," *History and Theory* 23 (1984) 1–33 [with bibliography]. He defends "narrativism" against the attacks of the "Annal school," among others.
3. For Jack and the Beanstalk, see Stith Thompson, *Motif-Index,* F 54.2; for the Fisherman's Wife, C 733.1.
4. G. Williams, *Tradition and Originality in Roman Poetry* (Oxford, 1968) 623.
5. The best general account is C. Lévi-Strauss, *Structural Anthropology,* 2 vols. (New York, 1963, 1976).
6. Stith Thompson, *Motif-Index,* collects an immense number of tales under the category "Reversal of Fortune": L 0 to L 399, esp. L 161, L 165.

BIBLIOGRAPHY

Altheim, F. *Literatur und Gesellschaft.* Vol. 2. Halle, 1950.
Aly, W. *Volksmärchen, Sage, und Novelle bei Herodot und seinen Zeitgenossen.* Göttingen, 1921; rpt. 1969.
Andrewes, A. *The Greek Tyrants.* London, 1956.
Armayor, O. K. "Did Herodotus Ever Go to the Black Sea?" *HSCP* 82 (1978) 45–62.
———. "Did Herodotus Ever Go to Egypt?" *JARCE* 15 (1980) 59–71.
———. "Sesostris and Herodotus' Autopsy of Thrace, Colchis, Inland Asia Minor, and the Levant." *HSCP* 84 (1980) 51–74.
Avery, H. C. "Herodotus' Picture of Cyrus." *AJP* 93 (1972) 529–546.
Bacon, H. *Barbarians in Greek Tragedy.* New Haven, 1961.
Baldry, H. C. *The Unity of Mankind in Greek Thought.* Cambridge, 1965.
Baldwin, B. "How Credulous Was Herodotus?" *G&R* 11 (1964) 167–177.
Ball, R. "Herodotus' List of the Spartans Who Died at Thermopylae." *MusAfr* 5 (1976) 1–8.
Barth, H. "Zur Bewertung und Auswahl des Stoffes durch Herodot (Die Begriffe, θῶμα, θωμάζω, und θωμαστός)." *Klio* 50 (1968) 93–110.

————. "Nochmals Herodot 1.8.3." *Philologus* 112 (1968) 288–291.

Benardete, S. *Herodotean Inquiries.* Hague, 1969.

Bickel, E. "Rekonstruktions-Versuch einer hellenistischen Gyges-Nysia-Tragödie." *RhM* 100 (1957) 141–152.

Bischoff, H. *Der Warner bei Herodot.* Leipzig, 1932.

Bornitz, H. F. *Herodot-Studien.* Berlin, 1968.

Bovon, A. "La représentation des guerriers perses et la notion de barbare dans la 1ʳᵉ moitié du Vᵉ siècle," *BCH* 87 (1963) 579–602.

Brown, T. S. "Herodotus and His Profession." *AHR* 59 (1954) 829–843.

La Bua, V. "Logos samio e storia samia in Erodoto." *MGR* 6 (1978) 1–88.

Burkert, W. "Iranisches bei Anaximandros." *RhM* 106 (1963) 97–134.

Bury, J. B. *Ancient Greek Historians.* New York, 1958.

Cobet, J. *Herodots Exkurse und die Frage der Einheit seines Werkes.* Weisbaden, 1971.

Cooper, G. L., III. "Intrusive Oblique Infinitives in Herodotus." *TAPA* 104 (1974) 23–76.

Davie, J. N. "Herodotus and Aristophanes on Monarchy." *G&R* 26 (1979) 160–168.

Diels, H. "Herodot und Hekataios." *Hermes* 22 (1887) 411–444.

Dihle, A. "Herodot und die Sophistik." *Philologus* 106 (1962) 207–220.

Diller, A. *Race Mixture Among the Greeks Before Alexander.* Urbana, 1937.

Diller, H. "Zwei Erzählungen des Lyders Xanthos." In *Navicula Chilonensis; Festschrift Jacoby.* Leiden, 1956.

————. "Die Hellenen-Barbaren Antithese im Zeitalter der Perserkrieg." In *Grecs et Barbares.* Fondation Hardt, Entretiens 8. Vandoeuvres, Genève, 1961.

Drews, R. "The First Tyrants in Greece." *Historia* 21 (1972) 129–144.

————. *The Greek Accounts of Eastern History.* Washington, D.C., 1973.

Edwards, G. P. *The Language of Hesiod in Its Traditional Context.* Oxford, 1971.

Ehrenberg, V. *The People of Aristophanes.* Oxford, 1951.

————. *The Greek State.* Oxford, 1960.

Erbse, H. "Der Erste Satz im Werke Herodots." In *Festschrift Bruno Snell,* 209–222. Munich, 1956.

_____. "Tradition und Form im Werke Herodots." *Gymnasium* 68 (1961) 239–257.

Evans, J. A. S. "The Dream of Xerxes and the 'Nomoi' of the Persians." *CJ* 57 (1961) 109–111.

_____. "Father of History or Father of Lies; the Reputation of Herodotus." *CJ* 64 (1968) 11–17.

_____. "Notes on the Debate of the Persian Grandees in Herodotus." *QUCC* 36 (1981) 69–84.

_____. *Herodotus.* Twayne's World Author Series, no. 645. Boston, 1982.

Fehling, D. *Die Quellenangaben bei Herodot: Studien zur Erzählkunst Herodots.* Berlin, 1971.

Ferguson, J. *Utopias of the Classical World.* London, 1975.

Ferrill, A. "Herodotus on Tyranny." *Historia* 27 (1978) 385–398.

Finley, M. I. *The Use and Abuse of History.* London, 1975.

Flory, S. "Arion's Leap: Brave Gestures in Herodotus." *AJP* 99 (1978) 411–421.

_____. "Laughter, Tears, and Wisdom in Herodotus." *AJP* 99 (1978) 145–153.

_____. "Who Read Herodotus' *Histories?*" *AJP* 101 (1980) 12–28.

Fornara, C. *Herodotus: An Interpretative Essay.* Oxford, 1971.

Forrest, W. G. "Herodotus and Athens." *Phoenix* 38 (1984) 1–11.

von Fritz, K. *Die Griechische Geschichtsschreibung.* 2 vols. Berlin, 1967.

Gigante, M. *Nomos Basileus.* Naples, 1956.

Gomperz, T. *Greek Thinkers.* Translated by L. Magnus. London, 1901.

Gould, J. "Law, Custom, and Myth: Women in Classical Athens." *JHS* 100 (1980) 38–59.

Grant, J. R. "Some Thoughts on Herodotus." *Phoenix* 37 (1983) 283–298.

Grote, G. *A History of Greece.* London, 1969, many reprints.

Groten, F. J., Jr. "Herodotus' Use of Variant Versions." *Phoenix* 17 (1963) 79–87.

Grundy, G. B. *The Great Persian War.* London, 1901.

Harder, R. "Herodot 1.8.3." In *Studies Presented to D. M. Robinson II,* edited by G. E. Mylonas and D. Raymond. St. Louis, 1953. (Also in Marg, 370–374.)

Hart, J. *Herodotus and Greek History.* London, 1982.

Hartog, F. *Le miroir d'Hérodote: Essai sur la représentation de l'autre.* Paris, 1980.

———. "Les amazones d'Hérodote: Inversions et tiers exclus." In
Pour Leon Poliakov: Le racisme. Mythes et Sciences, edited by M.
Olender, 177–186. Paris and Brussels, 1981.

Harvey, F. D. "The Political Sympathies of Herodotus." *Historia* 15
(1966) 254–255.

Havelock, E. A. *Preface to Plato.* Oxford, 1963.

Hirst, G. "Herodotus on Tyranny *versus* Athens and Democracy." In
her *Collected Classical Papers.* Oxford, 1938.

Hohti, P. "Über die Notwendigkeit bei Herodot." *Arctos* 9 (1975)
31–37.

Housman, A. E. "Fragment of a Greek Tragedy." *Cornhill Magazine,*
New Series 10 (1901) 444–445.

How, W. W., and J. Wells. *A Commentary on Herodotus.* 2 vols.
Oxford, 1928; rpt. 1957.

Hunter, V. *Past and Process in Herodotus and Thucydides.* Princeton,
1982.

Immerwahr, H. R. "Historical Action in Herodotus." *TAPA* 85
(1954) 16–45.

———. "Aspects of Historical Causation in Herodotus." *TAPA* 87
(1956) 241–280.

———. "The Samian Stories of Herodotus." *CJ* 52 (1957) 312–322.

———. "*Ergon:* History as Monument in Herodotus and
Thucydides." *AJP* 81 (1960) 261–290.

———. *Form and Thought in Herodotus.* Cleveland, 1966.

Jacoby, F. "Herodotus." In his *Griechische Historiker,* Stuttgart,
1956. (Also in *RE,* Supplement 2, Stuttgart, 1913, columns 205–
520.)

Jüthner, J. *Hellenen und Barbaren.* Leipzig, 1923.

Kagan, D. *The Great Dialogue: The History of Greek Political Thought
from Homer to Polybius.* New York, 1965.

Kennedy, G. *The Art of Persuasion in Greece.* Princeton, 1963.

Kirk, G. S. *The Nature of Greek Myths.* Harmondsworth, 1974.

Kirkwood, G. M. "Thucydides' Words for 'Cause.'" *AJP* 73 (1952)
37–61.

Lang, M. L. *Herodotean Narrative and Discourse.* Cambridge, Mass.,
1984.

Last, H. "ΑΙΘΙΟΠΕΣ ΜΑΚΡΟΒΙΟΙ." *CQ* 17 (1923) 35–36.

Lateiner, D. "A Note on the Perils of Prosperity in Herodotus."
RhM 125 (1982) 97–101.

Lattimore, R. "The Wise Advisor in Herodotus." *CP* 34 (1939) 24–
35.

―――. "The Composition of the History of Herodotus." *CP* 53 (1958) 9–21.

Lebeck, A. *The Oresteia.* Cambridge, Mass., 1971.

Lefkowitz, M. R. "Princess Ida and the Amazons, and a Women's College Curriculum." *TLS* 4104 (1981) 1399–1401.

Legrand, Ph.-E. *Hérodote: Histoires.* 11 vols. Paris, 1946–1956.

Lesky, A. "Das hellenistische Gyges Drama." *Hermes* 81 (1953) 1–10.

Lévi-Strauss, C. *Structural Anthropology.* 2 vols. New York, 1963, 1976.

von Leyden, W. M. "Spatium Historicum." *Durham University Journal* 11 (1949–1950) 89–104. (Excerpts in Marg, 169–184.)

Ligota, C. R. "Fact and Fiction in Antiquity." *Journal of the Warburg and Courtauld Institutes* 45 (1982) 1–13.

Linforth, I. M. "Herodotus' Avowal of Silence in His Account of Egypt." *UCPCP* 7 (1924) 269–292.

Lloyd, A. B. *Herodotus, Book II: Introduction.* Études préliminaires aux Religions orientales dans l'Empire Romain. Vol. 43. Leiden, 1975.

Lloyd, G. E. R. *Polarity and Analogy.* Cambridge, 1966.

Lloyd-Jones, H. *The Justice of Zeus.* Berkeley, 1971.

Lovejoy, A. O., and G. Boas. *Primitivism and Related Ideas in Antiquity.* Baltimore, 1935.

Luria, S. "Frauenpatriotismus und Sklavenemanzipation." *Klio* 26 (1933) 211–228.

Luther, W. "Der frühgriechische Wahrheitsgedanke im Lichte der Sprache." *Gymnasium* 65 (1958) 75–107.

Macan, R. W. *Herodotus: The Seventh, Eighth, and Ninth Books.* London, 1908.

Marg, W., ed. *Herodot: Eine Auswahl aus der neueren Forschung.* 3rd ed. Darmstadt, 1982.

Massaro, V. "Herodotus' Account of the Battle of Marathon and the Picture in the Stoa Poikile." *AC* 47 (1978) 458–475.

Maude, A., and J. L. Myres. "The Desert Pipe-Line in Herodotus 3.9." *CR* 60 (1946) 19.

Momigliano, A. "The Place of Herodotus in the History of Historiography." *History* 43 (1958) 1–13. (Also in *Secondo contributo alla storia degli studi classici,* 29–44. Rome, 1960.)

Montgomery, H. *Gedanke und Tat.* Stockholm, 1965.

Morrison, J. S. "The Place of Protagoras in Athenian Public Life." *CQ* 35 (1941) 1–16.

Murray, G. *Greek Studies.* Oxford, 1946.

Myres, J. L. *Herodotus: Father of History.* Oxford, 1953.

Nestle, W. *Vom Mythos zum Logos.* Stuttgart, 1942; rpt. 1966.

Olmstead, A. T. *History of the Persian Empire.* Chicago, 1948.

Ostwald, M. *Nomos and the Beginnings of Athenian Democracy.* Oxford, 1969.

Parry, A. M. "Thucydides' Historical Perspective." *YCS* 22 (1972) 49–61.

Pearson, L. *Early Ionian Historians.* Oxford, 1939.

———. "Credulity and Skepticism in Herodotus." *TAPA* 72 (1941) 333–355.

———. "*Prophasis* and *Aitia*." *TAPA* 83 (1952) 205–223.

Pembroke, S. "Women in Charge: The Function of Alternatives in Early Greek Tradition and the Ancient Idea of Matriarchy." *JWI* 30 (1967) 1–35.

Pippidi, D. M. "Sur la philosophie de l'histoire d'Hérodote." *Eirene* 1 (1960) 75–92.

Podlecki, A. J. "Herodotus in Athens?" In *Greece and the Eastern Mediterranean: Studies Presented to F. Schachermeyr on the Occasion of His Eightieth Birthday,* edited by K. H. Kinzl, 246–265. Berlin, 1977.

———. "Festivals and Flattery: The Early Greek Tyrants as Patrons of Poetry." *Athenaeum* 58 (1980) 371–395.

Pohlenz, M. *Herodot.* Stuttgart, 1961.

Pouncey, P. F. *The Necessities of War.* New York, 1980.

Powell, J. E. "Puns in Herodotus." *CR* 51 (1937) 103–105.

———. *The History of Herodotus.* Cambridge, 1939.

———. *A Lexicon to Herodotus.* 2nd ed. Hildesheim, 1960.

Pucci, P. *Hesiod and the Language of Poetry.* Baltimore, 1977.

Ravn, O. E. *Herodotus' Description of Babylon.* Translated by M. Tovberg-Jensen. Copenhagen, 1942.

Rawlinson, G. *History of Herodotus.* London, 1875.

Redfield, J. "Herodotus the Tourist." *CP* 80 (1985) 97–118.

Reinhardt, K. "Gyges und sein Ring." In *Vermächtnis der Antike,* edited by C. Becker, 175–183. Göttingen, 1960.

———. "Herodots Persergeschichten." In *Vermächtnis der Antike,* edited by C. Becker. Göttingen, 1960. (Also in Marg, 320–369.)

de Romilly, J. "La vengeance comme explication historique dans l'oeuvre d'Hérodote." *REG* 84 (1971) 314–337.

Rose, H. J. "Some Herodotean Rationalisms." *CQ* 34 (1940) 78–84.

Rossellini, M., and S. Saïd. "Usages des femmes et autres *nomoi* chez les 'sauvages' d'Hérodote: essai de lecture structurale." *ASNP* 8 (1978) 949–1005.

Ryberg, I. S. "Tacitus' Art of Innuendo." *TAPA* 73 (1942) 383–404.

Salmon, A. "L'expérience de Psammétique." *LEC* 24 (1956) 321–329.

Sayce, A. H. *The Ancient Empires of the East.* London, 1883.

Schadewaldt, W. "Herodot als erster Historiker." *Die Antike* 10 (1934) 144–168. (Also in Marg, 109–121.)

Schepens, G. "L'idéal de l'information complète chez les historiens grecs." *REG* 88 (1975) 81–93.

Schmid, W., and O. Stählin. *Geschichte der griechischen Literatur.* Vol. 1, pt. 2. Munich, 1934.

Schwabl, H. "Das Bild der fremden Welt bei den frühen Griechen." In *Grecs et Barbares.* Fondation Hardt 8. Vandoeuvres, Genève, 1961.

Sealey, R. "Thucydides, Herodotus, and the Causes of War." *CQ* 51 (1957) 1–12.

Shimron, B. "Πρῶτος τῶν ἡμεῖς ἴδμεν." *Eranos* 71 (1973) 45–51.

Shipp, G. P. *Nomos 'Law.'* Sydney, 1978.

Slater, P. *The Glory of Hera.* Boston, 1968.

Smith, K. F. "The Tale of Gyges and the King of Lydia I–II." *AJP* 23 (1902) 261–282, 362–387.

————. "The Literary Tradition of Candaules and Gyges." *AJP* 41 (1920) 1–37.

Spath, T. *Das Motiv der doppelten Beleuchtung bei Herodot.* Vienna, 1968.

Stahl, H.-P. "Herodots Gyges-Tragödie." *Hermes* 96 (1968) 385–400.

————. "Learning through Suffering? Croesus' Conversations in the History of Herodotus." *YCS* 24 (1975) 1–36.

Starr, C. G. "Ideas of Truth in Early Greece." *PP* 23 (1968) 348–359.

————. *The Awakening of the Greek Historical Spirit.* New York, 1968.

Stein, H. *Herodotos.* 9 vols. 1881–1896 and other dates. Rpt. 9 vols. in 5. Zurich, 1962–1969.

Stern, F., ed. *Varieties of History.* Cleveland, 1956.

Strasburger, H. "Herodot und das perikleische Athen." *Historia* 4 (1955) 1–25.

Stroheker, K. "Zu den Anfängen der monarchischen Theorie in der Sophistik." *Historia* 2 (1953–1954) 381–412.

Stubbings, F. H. "Xerxes and the Plane Tree." *G&R* 15 (1946) 63–67.

Thompson, S. *Motif-Index of World Folk-Literature.* Rev. ed. Bloomington, 1979.

Tyrrell, W. B. *Amazons, A Study in Athenian Mythmaking.* Baltimore, 1984.

Usener, H. "Milch und Honig." *RhM* 57 (1902) 177–195.

Verdin, H. "Hérodote historien? Quelques interprétations récentes." *AC* 44 (1975) 668–685.

Vernant, J. P. "Les troupeaux du soleil et la table du soleil." *REG* 85 (1972) xiv–xvii.

Wardman, A. E. "Herodotus on the Cause of the Greco-Persian Wars (Herodotus, I.5)." *AJP* 82 (1961) 133–150.

Waters, K. H. "Herodotus and the Ionian Revolt." *Historia* 19 (1970) 504–508.

———. *Herodotus the Historian.* Norman, 1985.

Webster, T. B. L. *Political Interpretations in Greek Literature.* Manchester, 1948.

Weiler, I. "Greek and Non-Greek World in the Archaic Period." *GRBS* 9 (1968) 21–29.

Wells, J. *Studies in Herodotus.* Oxford, 1923.

White, H. "The Question of Narrative in Contemporary Historical Theory." *History and Theory* 23 (1984) 1–33.

Williams, G. *Tradition and Originality in Roman Poetry.* Oxford, 1968.

Wolff, E. "Das Weib des Masistes." *Hermes* 92 (1964) 51–58. (Also in Marg, 668–678.)

Wood, H. *The Histories of Herodotus.* Hague, 1972.

Woodhouse, W. J. *The Composition of Homer's Odyssey.* Oxford, 1930.

INDEX OF REFERENCES TO HERODOTUS

INDEX

Stewart Flory is associate professor of classics at Gustavus Adolphus College in St. Peter, Minnesota. He received his Ph.D. from Yale University and has taught in the Classics Department at Amherst College and has been a Research Fellow and Senior Associate Member at the American School of Classical Studies in Athens. Currently he is a visiting scholar at the American Academy in Rome.

The manuscript was edited by Cathie Brettschneider. The book was designed by Don Ross. The typeface for the text and the display is Garamond. The book is printed on 55-lb. Glatfelter natural and is bound in Holliston Mills' Roxite A linen over binder's boards.

Manufactured in the United States of America.